Minimizing
Ministerial Mistakes
A Handbook For New Pastors

Dr. Ron Churchill

Minimizing Ministerial Mistakes: A Handbook For New Pastors

ISBN: Softcover 978-1-955581-40-0

Copyright © 2021 by Dr. Ron Churchill

All rights reserved. No part of this book may be reproduced or transmitted in any form or by any means, electronic or mechanical, including photocopying, recording, or by any information storage and retrieval system, without permission in writing from the publisher.

Parson's Porch Books is an imprint of Parson's Porch & Company (PP&C) in Cleveland, Tennessee. PP&C is an innovative organization which raises money by publishing books of noted authors, representing all genres. Its face and voice is **David Russell Tullock** (dtullock@parsonsporch.com).

Parson's Porch & Company *turns books into bread & milk* by sharing its profits with the poor.

www.parsonsporch.com

Minimizing Ministerial Mistakes

Contents

Foreword 7
Introduction 11
Chapter 1 15
   Going To A New Church
Chapter 2 21
   Scriptures You Have To Know
Chapter 3 30
   How To Make A Visitation List
Chapter 4 32
   How To Make An At-Home Visit
Chapter 5 39
   How To Share The Gospel
Chapter 6 42
   How To Work With Staff
Chapter 7 47
   How To Develop A Sermon
Chapter 8 50
   Where To Get Illustrations
Chapter 9 51
   What To Say At A Funeral
Chapter 10 56
   How To Show Love For The People
Chapter 11 59
   How To Motivate Sunday Small Groups
Chapter 12 62
   How To Make A Hospital Visit
Chapter 13 66
   How To Reach Out To Single Adults
Chapter 14 90
   How To Show Love To Senior Adults

Chapter 15 97
    About My Schedule
Chapter 16 100
    Personal Integrity
Chapter 17 104
    The Power Of Prayer
Chapter 18 107
    The Pastor's Prayers Are Important
Chapter 19 112
    Dealing With Problems In Your Church
Chapter 20 120
    Don't Run Off All The People In The Church That You Don't Like
Chapter 21 125
    Keep The Main Thing The Main Thing
Chapter 22 130
    Great Ideas To Get You Going
Chapter 23 137
    Christians Must Stand And Fight Against Socialism
About the Author

Foreword

In one book **Dr. Ron Churchill** shares the wisdom gathered in almost 60 years of experience as pastor of Baptist churches. Everything a new or young pastor needs to know about building a church and relating to people in the pew is included. Read this book and you will know the essentials of pastoral ministry, working with senior adults, single adults, and Sunday School classes. Dr. Churchill outlines in clever ways how to deal with difficult people, and how to help deacons and lay leadership become successful in the church's programs and ministries.

Dr. Churchill is candid, humorous and uses straight talk about many issues, problems, and opportunities that a young pastor will encounter. His specialty is evangelism, specifically, leading someone to a personal relationship with Christ, and gives heart-felt stories from his experience. Pastoral counseling, conducting funerals, how to make hospital visits, the minister's personal finances and investments, personal integrity in the ministry, and even how to know when it is time to seek another leadership position – all covered in details in this book, all of which comes from the personal experience of a successful pastor. The author even details the scriptures one must have memorized which are useful in many circumstances in ministry and outlines his secret to a vibrant pulpit ministry.

This is a must read for young pastors, and nothing else will compare to the wealth of knowledge Dr. Churchill shares. This is the "idea book" of practical advice and suggestions written in plain language with meaningful stories and illustrations.

R. Page Fulgham, Th.D.
Retired Baptist Pastor, Guest Professor Baugh Center of Baptist Leadership, Mercer University

Dr. Ron Churchill has had a very interesting life of ministry in his 57 years of service. He has pastored small and mega churches. In each of his places of service they had to increase the parking a lot.

This book is written for pastors who have just finished college or seminary or have just come out of the secular world. He has tried to help new pastors avoid unnecessary mistakes in their new church. Specific areas where problems can mushroom quickly are dealt with throughout this book.

In the days of dealing with Coronavirus and our great need of church revitalization, these ideas can be very helpful. Dr. Churchill felt called to ministry in his second year at Baylor University and he started with two small country churches. Later on in his ministry he served at the First Baptist Church in Plant City, Florida. God blessed that work and the church doubled in size over his 21 years pastoring there. With 3,500 members, the church ministers in various ways and has continued to grow after his retirement.

Throughout his ministry, Dr. Churchill has reached out, particularly to single adults and senior adults. In many churches, these two groups have been overlooked. Since over half of the adult population in America are single, those groups really need revitalization. Having singles and senior adults joining weekly, every church will feel new life and vitality. This book will be greatly helpful in that regard.

Dr. Danny L. Morris, Sr.
Association Missionary Strategist
President of Biblical Leadership Institute
Pastor of 3Streams.Today Online Church

In 1990 I became the pastor of a church in Plant City, Florida that was struggling through several controversial issues. I was twenty-six years old leading my first full-time congregation. Ron immediately became a good friend and without even knowing it, he also became a fabulous mentor. For more than five years we would eat lunch together at least once a week. Those lunches provided a wealth of pastoral advice that guided me through many problematic situations.

I told Ron, on more than one occasion, that he needed to write all this down in a book one day. He did! And this work, Handbook For New Pastors, is the result.

Young and older pastors entering the ministry, trying to navigate the treacherous waters of the local church, will find this practical advice from Ron very beneficial and a big help in avoiding many pitfalls that naturally exist. Ron provides a wealth of practical information and great, biblical advice for the pastor that genuinely wants to make a difference for the Kingdom of God.

Dr. Joel Samuels, Pastor
First Baptist Church, Guntersville, Alabama

Ron Churchill has been a friend of mine for over 50 years. Our friendship started with our mutual enrollment at Southwestern Baptist Theological Seminary in Ft. Worth, Texas. Later he was my "best man" at my wedding to Joan Harriet Drake 51 years ago.

Ron has enjoyed a very effective and joyful ministry for these many years.

He has been especially effective in growing Single Adult Ministries and building strong churches through his God given calling!

This book has grown out of his many years of Christian Ministry. It is an insightful confession of mistakes to be avoided. The book is especially helpful for Pastors who want to avoid mistakes in pastoring.

I have admired Ron's consistent and effective ministry throughout his entire life. As one gets older, having a comrade in the 'Good Lord's Army' is especially helpful and encouraging to continue forward in the ministry of our Lord and Savior, Jesus Christ.

James R. Patterson
PH.D Systematic Theology Southwestern Baptist Theological Seminary, Former Professor, Golden Gate Baptist Theological Seminary

Introduction

Many experiences shape our lives and our ministries. I accepted Jesus as my Savior when I was 15 years old through a softball coach who also happened to be a youth minister at the local Baptist church. I felt the Lord's leading me into ministry and even preached twice on student day at our church. Even though I was reared in the conservative church-going community of Chattanooga, Tennessee; my parents were not religious people. They were, however, big on education. When I finished high school, I wanted to go to a Baptist college and because of the strong academic component, my father agreed for me to attend Baylor University in Waco, Texas. Just as I got on the train to leave for Baylor, my parents told me to do well because I could not come back home to live.

A few months after arriving at Baylor I decided to run for president of the freshman class. I was elected president and called my parents to tell them about it. My dad cussed me out. He said, "We are not paying for you to fool around out there." He had helped me with my tuition. I thought about that call and three days later, I called my dad and told him not to help me financially any longer.

While at Baylor University I pastored a small country church in White Mound, Texas. (Dr. W.A. Criswell was the pastor of that church when he was a student at Baylor.) I also was a security guard on an armored truck and cut meat at a business that supplied food for schools in the area. Every opportunity that I could preach, I accepted. I was able to preach over 200 student led revivals throughout college and seminary. Working three jobs at the same time, studying, and participating in any ministry opportunity that came my way was difficult. I had very little money, drove junky cars, and had a limited social life.

I got involved in a ministry at Baylor called "Friday Night Missions." Baylor students would go out and minister with very poor minority children. It was like having Vacation Bible School every Friday night all year long. I loved it and we all loved those kids. I had never done anything like that before. At first, I worked in one mission place as a helper, then after a few months, I became the leader. About six months later I became the leader of the whole program with multiple locations. I talked to a lot of kids about Jesus and sometimes their parents as well. I loved it all.

I then pastored another country church for two years and afterward went to Southern Methodist University in Dallas to be the Baptist Student Union director. The program was set up to lead the college students to Christ. I worked with about 200 students, trying to help them grow in their faith. Every morning during the week, I went to Southwestern Baptist Theological Seminary. In the afternoons and evenings, I related to the students at SMU.

After finishing my master's degree at Southwestern, I went to New Orleans Baptist Theological Seminary to complete my doctoral work. To help pay for my studies, I worked at a plant on the Mississippi River and guarded cars at night for an automobile company. I was able to study while I sat in my car with a gun and didn't let anyone go onto the property.

For most of my ministry I was the lead pastor but was also a single adult pastor in three different churches and was the leading single adult speaker in the U.S. for over 20 years. It was unique that I did not get married till I was 50 years old and could relate to the issues facing single adults in a very personal way. In 1993, I met and married a lovely Christian lady. Cindy was working as the director of an at-risk Christian girls' home. She ministered to girls that were out of sorts with their parents, school, and society. Cindy led hundreds of girls to the Lord in her 37 years of ministry. We both understood the demands of ministry and could help each other as we served the Lord. Cindy and I retired a few years ago. God has been so good to us.

Coming from an unchurched home taught me to not assume that people understand spiritual words and concepts. It helped me to simplify salvation and faith so that anyone can understand. It also helped me to relate to more people with compassion and meet them where they are to lead them to Jesus.

Working my way through school taught me a good work ethic. It also helped me know how hard it is to run a business or build up investments so that you could later take care of your bills and your family. Everyone needs to be ready for the real world when they finish school. It helped me to not take blessings like financial support and people for granted. I never forgot what it was like to struggle and that has made me a good steward of the gifts, spiritual and physical, that the Lord had given me.

Pastoring churches always was a great joy for me. I tried to love God and love the people. That plan worked well for me.

This book is written to help pastors as they go to a new church. I am sharing lessons learned through almost six decades of experience in ministry that isn't necessarily something learned in class. I hope that this can be a blessing to you as the Lord uses your unique gifts and background to serve Him and His people. I ask that you would pass on this book to another new pastor. It might be a tremendous blessing for them.

Chapter 1
Going To A New Church

In my 57 years of pastoring, I was the "New Minister" seven times. Sometimes I was awful at assimilating into the church body in the first few months or even the first year. I made a lot of mistakes.

In my first church I was 19 and still going to college. Among the mistakes I made, I forgot to join the church. In the third week an elderly gentleman in the church asked me if I liked the church. I said, "Yes, I do. I love it." He said, "Well, when do you plan to join?" The next Sunday I joined.

Sometimes we are the new minister when we finish college or when we finish seminary. Sometimes we go into ministry at mid-life, or when we retire from a secular job. Whenever it is, being the new minister is a difficult and arduous transition. This book is purposed to help the young pastor to have a successful start in ministry. We will look at twenty-three aspects that you will have to deal with in your first days at a new place of ministry. These include encountering new people that you don't know, the expectations from the new congregation, and working with new staff and leadership.

Every church is different. My first little church was way out in the country. The people knew about farming and how to deal with cattle and horses and pigs. I grew up in Chattanooga and I knew nothing about any of the things they knew a lot about.

A very nice family invited me to lunch with their family my third week working there as their pastor.

In the course of lunch, the conversation turned to their cattle. They talked about that for a while. Then I asked the dumbest question a city boy could ask. I asked, "What is the difference between a steer and a cow?" This family had two children in grammar school and they both started laughing when I asked my question. I know the parents thought, "Our pastor is ignorant." I learned a lot about animals at that church. I also learned about maize. I had never heard of maize.

There were a lot of retired teachers in that tiny town. Every one of the retired teachers wanted to tell me about their field of teaching. I learned a lot of things I didn't care about, like trigonometry and how to deal with snakes.

As you go to your new church or to your first church, you must consider that everyone comes from a different background. Your job is not to stay away from difficult people. Your job is to help people grow in Christ. Your job is to help people be more loving to everybody. Prepare yourself for wild questions and off-the-wall statements. Sometimes your best answer is to say, "Let me look that up in the Bible." Once you have found a verse in the Bible that speaks to that bizarre issue, explain to them the verse in a loving way.

Everyone in your new church wants to know what you think about the Bible and what you know about the Bible. If you let everyone know what you believe about politics, you are going to alienate about half the congregation. I preached against socialism but did not do it until I was there at least three years. Your new church needs to learn quickly that you love Jesus, you love the Bible, and you love them. If you can really live out those three things, you will do well in your church.

While visiting patients in the hospital, on more than one occasion I have been asked to look at various places on a person's body. They want to show me how gory some place is after their operation. I didn't want to look at any of that, and you won't either; but get ready because numerous people will ask you to look. I have been asked various questions about sexual issues. Get ready for that as well. I tried to recommend counselors who were specifically trained to answer those kinds of questions. People will ask you if everyone has a soul. Believe me, racism is not dead. People will ask you about new fads. Some will tell you that only Paul's writings are relevant for today. That, of course, is inane but you want to deal with that with Scripture and not by arguing.

You should plan to go to the hometown's biggest events. You might want to serve on the boards of other local organizations. You should go to some city council meetings and get to know all the city council members. Visit people that live close to your home. People tell other people if the new guy is reaching out.

Find something at your new church that needs to look better. Get four or five people from the church to help you paint it. Find everything that is broken at the church and get it fixed.

Mention in church the names of the people who helped. Get some volunteers to pick up trash early on Sunday morning. Get the staff to help you pick up the trash around the church during the work week. Don't let the church people think that you see yourself as high and mighty and way too important to move chairs or help clean up after a meeting. Your first few months at your new church are very important. Some people make up their minds about things the first day. Smile a lot.

The following list of Do's and Don'ts have been very helpful to me throughout my ministry.

> • Don't start with the attitude that says, "I'm going to show them who's the boss around here."

I would make no major changes my first year. You actually become the pastor of the church around your third year there. Remember, every dog has its fleas. No matter how bad a certain staff person may be, some people think he or she is the greatest person in the world. Be particularly careful with older staff members. If you fire or undermine an older staff member, the whole senior adult group might turn against you.

> • Don't change music styles overnight.

If a church has had one style of music for years, you should move slowly in changing to another style. Perhaps you should go to a blended service for at least a year. Don't think that just because you change the music style hundreds of young people are going to come. There needs to be an effective youth minister in place and a supportive group of workers.

- Do park as far away from the front door of the church as much as possible.

If there is a designated spot for the pastor to park, get rid of that immediately. If anyone questions you about this, tell them the places close to the church should be open for the senior adults and visitors. Also, encourage your staff and deacons to park as far away from the door as possible.

- Don't refer to your previous church or churches all the time.

That gets old in a hurry. People don't care about what you did at your last church. The people want you to focus on your current church.

- Do become a part of your new community.

Go to some of the high school games and root for the home team. Maybe have a day where you honor the local football team or track team or whatever team in your Sunday morning service and serve a nice lunch for them after the service. Put up some school banners. If there is a local annual charity or positive community event, try to be a part of it and affirm the members of your church who are involved. It can be a great testimony for your church and way to draw in new members through those relationships. Whatever you do, **never** show resentment of the time spent serving these different community events. It will make you look small and take away from building up the church. Also, be careful to not criticize local businesses or large organizations. Your people may be employees of those organizations like teachers in the public school system or managers of the local grocery store. Stay positive and focus on things that lift up your people and draw them closer to Jesus.

Chapter 2
Scriptures You Have To Know

Some member of your new church will come up to you and ask, "Where is that verse that says, "While we were yet sinners Christ died for us?" You have two answers to that question. You can say, "Let's step into the library and look at a concordance; you can find out where any verse is by looking up a few key words in the concordance." Or you can say, "That verse is Romans 5:8."

You will be asked in your ministry <u>many times</u> where a particular verse is. Many times, you won't know. You will know how to finish the verse as they start it, but you won't be able to say it is in Matthew or John or Ephesians. I have been embarrassed many times in this over the years.

It will be helpful to you in many situations to know the most popular verses in the Bible. Your congregation loves to hear you quote Scripture and give the reference. I have listed the most used and useful verses. If you know these, you will be praised as a biblical scholar. The following Bible quotes are from the New King James translation.

> <u>John 3:16</u> For God so loved the world that He gave His only begotten Son that whosoever believes in Him should not perish but have everlasting life.

> <u>John 14:1-6</u> Let not your heart be troubled. You believe in God, believe also in me. In my Father's

house are many mansions; if it were not so, I would have told you. I go to prepare a place for you. And if I go and prepare a place for you, I will come again and receive you unto myself, that where I am there you may be also. And where I go you know, and the way you know. Thomas said to Jesus, "Lord, we do not know where You are going, so how can we know the way?" Jesus said to him, "I am the Way, the Truth and the Life. No one comes to the Father except through Me."

Psalm 23

23 The LORD *is* my shepherd;
I shall not want.
² He makes me to lie down in green pastures;
He leads me beside the still waters.
³ He restores my soul;
He leads me in the paths of righteousness
For His name's sake.

⁴ Yea, though I walk through the valley of the shadow of death,
I will fear no evil;
For You *are* with me;
Your rod and Your staff, they comfort me.

⁵ You prepare a table before me in the presence of my enemies;
You anoint my head with oil;
My cup runs over.

⁶ Surely goodness and mercy shall follow me
All the days of my life;
And I will dwell in the house of the LORD
Forever.

Psalm 118:24 This is the day the Lord has made. I will rejoice and be glad in it.

Proverbs 3:5-6 Trust in the Lord with all your heart and lean not on your own understanding. In all your ways acknowledge Him and He shall direct your paths.

Jeremiah 29:11 "For I know the plans I have for you," declares the Lord, "plans to prosper you and not harm you, plans to give you hope and a future."

Micah 6:8 What does the Lord require of you? To act justly, and to love mercy, and to walk humbly with your God.

Matthew 6:33 Seek first the kingdom of God and His righteousness, and all these things shall be added to you.

Matthew 5, 6 and 7 The Sermon On the Mount

Matthew 28:16-20 The Great Commission

Acts 1:8 But ye shall receive power after that the Holy Spirit will come upon you and you shall be witnesses unto Me both in Jerusalem and in all Judea, and in Samaria and unto the uttermost parts of the earth.

Acts 4:12 Salvation is found in no one else, for there is no other name under heaven given to men by which we must be saved.

Romans 3:23 For all have sinned and come short of the glory of God.

Romans 5:8 But God commended His love toward us in that while we were yet sinners, Christ died for us.

Romans 6:23 For the wages of sin is death, but the gift of God is eternal life through Jesus Christ our Lord.

Romans 8:28 And we know that all things work together for good to them that love God, to them who are called according to His purpose.

Romans 8:31 If God be for us, who can be against us?

Romans 10:9-10 That if thou shalt confess with thy mouth the Lord Jesus, and shalt believe in thine heart that God has raised Him from the dead, thou shalt be saved, for with the heart man believeth unto righteousness, and with the mouth confession is made unto salvation.

Romans 12:1-5 I beseech you therefore, brethren, by the mercies of God, that you present your bodies as a living sacrifice, holy, acceptable unto God, which is your reasonable service. And be not conformed to this world, but be ye transformed by the renewing of your mind, that you may prove what is that good and acceptable and perfect will of God. For I say through the grace given unto me, to every man that is among you, not to think of himself more highly than he ought to think but to think soberly, according as God hath dealt to every man the measure of faith. For as we have many members in one body and all members have not the same office, so we, being many, are one body in Christ, and every one members one of another.

I Corinthians 13:4-8, 13 Love suffers long and is kind; love does not envy; love does not parade itself, is not puffed up. Love does not behave rudely, does not seek its own; is not provoked; thinks no evil; does not rejoice in iniquity, but rejoices in the truth; bears all things; believes all things, hopes all things, endures all things. Love never fails. But whether there are prophecies, they will fail; whether there are tongues, they will cease; whether there is knowledge, it will vanish away....... [13] And now abide faith, hope love, these three; but the greatest of these *is* love.

II Corinthians 5:17   Therefore if any man be in Christ, he is a new creation; old things are passed away; behold, all things are become new.

II Corinthians 6:2   Behold, now is the accepted time; behold now is the day of salvation.

Galatians 5:22-23   But the fruit of the Spirit is love, joy, peace, patience, kindness, goodness, faith, meekness, self-control; against such there is no law.

Galatians 6:7   Be not deceived, God is not mocked, for whatever a man soweth, that shall he also reap.

Galatians 6:9   Let us not grow weary in well doing, for in due season we shall reap if we faint not.

Ephesians 2:89   For by grace are ye saved through faith, and that not of yourselves; it is the gift of God, not of works, lest any man should boast.

Philippians 4:6   Be anxious for nothing, but in everything, by prayer and supplication, with thanksgiving, let your requests be made known to God.

Philippians 4:8   Finally, brethren, whatever things are true, whatever things are noble, whatever things are just, whatever things are pure, whatever things are lovely, whatever things are of good report, if there is any virtue and if there is anything praiseworthy—meditate on these things.

Philippians 4:13 I can do all things through Christ who strengthens me.

II Timothy 1:7 For God has not given us the spirit of fear, but of power, and of love, and of a sound mind.

II Timothy 2:15 Be diligent to present yourself approved to God, a worker who does not need to be ashamed, rightly dividing the word of truth.

II Timothy 3:16 All Scripture is given by inspiration of God, and is profitable for doctrine, for reproof, for correction, for instruction in righteousness.

Hebrews 9:27 It is appointed unto men once to die, but after that the judgment.

Hebrews 11:6 But without faith it is impossible to please God, for he who comes to God must believe that He is, and that He is a rewarder of those who diligently seek God.

James 5:16 Confess your trespasses to one another, and for one another, that you may be healed. The effectual, fervent prayer of a righteous man avails much.

I Peter 3:15 But sanctify the Lord God in your hearts, and always be ready to give a defense to everyone who asks you a reason for the hope that is in you, with meekness and fear.

I Peter 5:7   Casting all your care upon Him, for He cares for you.

I John 1:8-9   If we say that we have no sin, we deceive ourselves and the truth is not in us. If we confess our sins, He is faithful to forgive us and to cleanse us from all unrighteousness.

Exodus 20:3-17 The Living Bible translation

(The Ten Commandments)

³ "You may worship no other god than me.

⁴ "You shall not make yourselves any idols: no images of animals, birds, or fish. ⁵ You must never bow or worship it in any way; for I, the Lord your God, am very possessive. I will not share your affection with any other god!

"And when I punish people for their sins, the punishment continues upon the children, grandchildren, and great-grandchildren of those who hate me; ⁶ but I lavish my love upon thousands of those who love me and obey my commandments.

⁷ "You shall not use the name of Jehovah your God irreverently, nor use it to swear to a falsehood. You will not escape punishment if you do.

⁸ "Remember to observe the Sabbath as a holy day. ⁹ Six days a week are for your daily duties and your regular work, ¹⁰ but the seventh day is a day of Sabbath rest before the Lord your God. On that day you are to do no work of any kind, nor shall your son, daughter, or slaves—whether men or women—or your cattle or your house guests. ¹¹ For in six days the Lord made the heaven, earth, and sea, and everything in them, and rested the seventh day; so he blessed the Sabbath day and set it aside for rest.

¹² "Honor your father and mother, that you may have a long, good life in the land the Lord your God will give you.

¹³ "You must not murder.

¹⁴ "You must not commit adultery.

¹⁵ "You must not steal.

¹⁶ "You must not lie.

¹⁷ "You must not be envious of your neighbor's house, or want to sleep with his wife, or want to own his slaves, oxen, donkeys, or anything else he has."

Chapter 3
How To Make A Visitation List

This is a very important task for every minister and every Bible study leader. In over five decades of pastoring churches, I have seen many programs come and go related to gathering information, visitation, and sharing the gospel. Although all these programs have their strengths and weaknesses, all must include the following to be effective.

As the visitor comes in any of the doors of the church there should be a church member with a short form to fill out. On the form have places where the visitor can fill in their name, address, and phone number. If you ask for a lot of information from the visitor, they will probably not fill out anything. Ask them to fill in the sheet and hand it to you or put it in the offering plate as it is passed during the worship service. You must train your members to greet those whom they do not know and ask them before the service begins to fill out a sheet (the one that was offered to them at the door).

The visitation sheet should include:

• List the names, addresses and phone numbers of recent visitors. If special information about visitors is known, put it on the sheet as well.
• Have a place on the sheet for pending surgeries and another place for praise and prayer requests.
• Have an open section for messages to the pastors and deacons.

Within the week, one of the ministers should visit every visitor. The next week a Bible study leader or a deacon should visit all the visitors. All reports and information should be given to the senior minister or administrative assistant.

Chapter 4
How To Make An At-Home Visit

You start out by ringing the doorbell and moving back from the door as far as possible. It gives the people a chance to see you through the door or one of the windows. Give people time to walk from the back of the house to the front door.

If people ask, "Who is it?" tell them your name in a loud voice and the name of your church. Say something positive like, "We are thrilled you visited our church." If they open their door, once again say, "I'm so-and-so from (your church name)." Since you look very different without a suit on or very different from what you looked like the day before, say something about you being the pastor of the church. I do not carry a big black Bible with me.

The first thing I say is their name, "James, we are so glad you visited our church. Do you have friends at (your church name)?" Their answer gives you a lot of information which you want to remember and write down on your visitation sheet when you get back to your car. If there are two people in the home, call both names a couple of times before you leave. If they give evidence in conversation to be Christian people, as I leave, I lead in a prayer calling both of their names again.

If there is something different or unusual in the home, I ask about it. If there is a dog or cat in the house, you should be very friendly toward them. I don't tell them this, but I don't get along well with cats. They make me sneeze.

If the people are new to town, I tell them about our best local restaurants and I tell them of a good dentist and a good doctor. I tell them about our town and our church. I tell them about our small groups and our special activities. I ask them if they like to sing in the choir. If they do like to sing, I give their names and phone number to our Minister of Music when I get back to the church. That call ought to be made that day.

The turning point in the conversation comes when I ask them if they have ever been to a Baptist church before. If they say they were a <u>member</u> of a Baptist church somewhere, I do not present the Gospel to them.

If they say they were members of some non-evangelical church, I move toward presenting the Gospel. At this point I ask them, "Was there ever a time in your life when you personally asked Jesus to come into your heart and be your Savior?" If they say no, then I present the Gospel and try to lead them to Jesus. If they say yes, I say, "I hope I haven't taken up too much of your day and I really hope you will be back the next Sunday." The next week, whether they come or not, I send a staff member or church visitor to that home. I call them the second week and just touch base with them.

I write down on my church bulletin early Sunday morning the names of all the people I have visited and the ones I hope will join. This gets their names in my mind as I walk around and greet people before the church service begins.

Don't be discouraged! Sometimes the Holy Spirit has already prepared the way and you are just the "Closer". When I was pastoring in Fayetteville, Georgia, we had visitation on Monday night. I was always there to take someone with me and train them how to visit a church prospect and, hopefully, how to lead someone to Christ.

On one Monday night there was a new church member there wanting to learn how to make a visit. I really didn't know him, but I asked him to go with me. We took two names and started driving to see the first prospect. We got lost. There was no GPS system back then. We drove around, but we just couldn't find the street we wanted. As we were driving around, it started getting dark.

We saw a house on a little hill that had on a lot of lights. I told my visiting partner I was going to drive up the driveway and ask the people that lived there where our street was. We pulled up close to the front door and a man came out to meet us. Before I could say anything, the man that lived there asked, "Are you a pastor?" I said, "Yes, I am." I noticed he looked like he had been crying. He said, "I have been praying that a pastor would come." As the evening went on, we knew the whole night was a miracle.

He invited us into his home. All the lights were on, but there was no furniture in the house. There were no pictures or curtains or chairs or tables. The house was barren. The homeowner asked us to sit down. The three of us sat down on the floor. The man was crying. We told him our names and which church we were from. He said, "God brought you both here." Then he started crying again. He told us his sad story.

He had left on a business trip for four days. As soon as he left, his wife started selling things. She, obviously, had a plan for her actions. He called every night and she told him everything was going well.

She sold everything in the house except the phone. She knew when he was coming back home and he found the house empty. She sold one of their cars and took all of their money out of the bank. As he told us the whole story, we were about to cry with him. He had called the police, but there had been no follow up.

I led us in a prayer for him and his wife. He started crying again. I talked to him about the Lord. He had gone to church as a boy, but had not grown in his faith. I talked to him about really committing himself to the Lord. He was open to that and I led him through the sinner's prayer. He accepted Christ as his Lord.

My ministry partner and I left, and he said, "This was the first time in my life I have been present when someone accepted Christ." He acknowledged that this was a great experience to see another man's life changed.

We then went to our second visit. The middle-aged lady was happy to see us. We sat down and began to talk with her. Her reason for putting a note in the offering plate as it went by on Sunday morning was that she was afraid her two boys were not going to go to heaven. The boys were 17 and 19.

As we visited with the lady, she shared with us that her husband had left nine years earlier. She was really not committed to the Lord and was not sure of her own salvation, but she knew enough about Jesus to know that her boys needed the Savior. She had gone to church as a child but had never taken her boys on a regular schedule.

I talked with her about her faith, and she wanted to be sure of her salvation so she could be a better witness to her boys. I told her about how the Bible was filled with prophecy and how all of those promises were fulfilled. I told her about how Jesus and Paul had promised for believers an eternity in heaven and not a moment in hell. I took her through the sinner's prayer and she accepted Christ as her Savior. We talked for about fifteen more minutes and were on our way to the front door when her oldest son came through the door. His mother introduced us to him and we all sat down to talk.

Her older son looked like an athlete and during our talk with him I told him my softball coach led me to Christ. I mentioned I thought he looked like an athlete. I told him I lettered in five sports in high school. It impressed him that I lettered in boxing and wrestling.

I told him about his mother trusting Jesus to be her Savior. She said, "Yes, I did and you need to do it as well." She started crying and put her arm around him. He was very open to my gospel presentation. Eventually, I led him in the sinner's prayer, and he trusted in Christ. The four of us visited for about thirty minutes and I told him about our teams at the church and told him he would love the softball team. He was very nice, and his mother was very happy.

As we went together to the front door, the younger son came home. The older brother said to his younger brother, "Come on in. We are all getting saved tonight." The younger brother had never gone to church, so I talked with him about our church for about forty-five minutes. The mother and the older brother listened carefully to all I said. I mentioned to the younger brother that he was quite handsome. I said a lot of the cute girls at our church would love to meet him. The younger brother was open to the gospel. I told him about the rich young ruler in the Bible and what a terrible mistake he had made in not trusting in Jesus as his Savior. I talked with him about the billions of people that had realized how important Jesus was.

I told him his mother and his older brother were going to heaven. I told him it would be wonderful if all three of them could be in heaven together. I said many of his friends would be there. I told him to read the third chapter of John in the New Testament over and over again until he completely understood every word. I gave him my card and told him to call me if he had any questions about anything. I told him I wanted to be his friend forever. The mother started crying again and all three of them hugged and kissed each other. I took him through the sinner's prayer and he committed himself to Christ. Then everyone cried and we were all hugging each other.

It was completely dark outside, and I realized we had been there for a long time. As we were leaving, my visiting partner was just in awe over what had happened that night. He said, "God had to be happy about what had happened tonight." I said, "Yes, God was very happy about tonight." I said, "God is happy about you being a part of all of this. Do it again and again for the glory of God."

I will never forget that night. Not every visitation night is that dramatic but when one avails him/herself, the Holy Spirit will operate in large and small ways.

Chapter 5
How To Share The Gospel

Call the person by name and attempt to get to know them before you start promoting salvation. Don't start with Romans 10:13, but you might end with it. It is a great scripture to close your conversation. Romans 10:9-10 is a very good scripture to explain and promote. Don't rush the person. Make sure they are with you as you go through the text. Ask for questions. Go over the text again. Don't assume that they understand what you are talking about. Many people come from a completely different background.

Between 13 and 14 years of age, I was going to a Presbyterian church. They had hayrides for the young people which I loved. Every year they also had a retreat in the mountains about 50 miles from where I grew up in Chattanooga. We had a lot of fun on those retreats. We played basketball, softball, and there were some small boats to use along the river beside the retreat center. Each night we would conclude the day with a time around a bonfire where all of us would sit around in a circle. The church staff member would give a devotional and then ask for someone to give a testimony. The girl that I liked very much stood up and gave a great testimony about how she became a Christian. I was very impressed with how she spoke and what she said. I thought I ought to have a testimony too. That night after everyone in my cabin had gone to bed, I decided to go down to the edge of the river. I just had on shorts and a t-shirt. It was cold. I spoke out loud trying to communicate with God. I said, "I want to be a Christian and I want a good testimony". I didn't hear any voice or see anything in the sky. I had heard the story a number of times at church how the Lord had spoken to Paul on the Damascus Road. That's what I wanted. I thought maybe I should yell. Louder than the time before I said, "I want to be a Christian and I want a good testimony". I still heard no voice and didn't see anything in the sky. It was cold out there. I thought, "I'm going to give God a few more minutes, then I am going back inside".

About a year later I started going to the Baptist church because they had the best softball team and I loved playing softball. The youth minister had talked to me about becoming a Christian after some of our softball games. He was a great man and really loved all of us kids. One Sunday night our regular pastor was not there, and the youth minister preached the sermon. At the conclusion of his sermon, he said, "If you are waiting on a white light in the sky or an audible voice, you don't have to have that to make a profession of faith". I felt God touching my heart, I slipped down the aisle, and became a Christian that night. I was baptized the next week and became very active in the church throughout my high school years.

If the person is having difficulty professing their faith, tell them an illustration. Tell them about two people wanting to get married but having difficulty nailing it down. Say, "Dating is wonderful, but it is different from being married. To be married you have to seal the deal. You have to ask this person to marry you and they have to answer in the affirmative. You both must have commitment and follow through. In trusting Christ as your Savior, you have to take a stand, you have to have commitment." Tell them about all the believers that will be with them in heaven forever.

Say, "Are you ready to commit yourself to Christ?" Repeat after me. "Dear Lord, I know that I am a sinner. I know the only way I can be saved is to place my faith in Jesus. Dear Lord, I want to do that right now."

After the person commits their life to Christ, say, "God bless you and welcome to the family of God." Tell them to get into a small group so that they can grow in faith. Follow up with the group leader to make sure that they are connected. Tell them you will be there for them. Tell them to share their faith with friends and family.

If the person emotionally breaks down somewhere quote Romans 3:23 and then Romans 5:8 and Romans 6:23. If the person gives some nebulous answer like "I have always been a Christian" or "my whole family are Christians," say, "We believe trusting in Christ is a thing you do once in life and happens at a very definite time and place. Please let this be your time and place. Let this be a moment when you change from sin and selfishness to love in Jesus. I am praying for you as I suspect others are as well. Let this be your day of victory."

Chapter 6
How To Work With Staff

Before I give methodologies for working with staff, let me present ideas about hiring staff. If you are the new pastor, there might be other new staff coming onboard soon.

Many times another pastor will hear about you wanting an additional staff person and they will call you to recommend a friend of theirs. Many times that pastor will call some of his pastor friends and ask them to call you about the same person. All of a sudden you have numerous pastors recommending the same person to you. You then feel like this must be God's will.

Some pastors recommend a friend of theirs who has been fired from a church because of moral misbehavior or financial difficulties or other difficult situations. We all want to give another person a second chance, particularly if they are a friend of ours, but you want to know the whole situation and what healing there has been before you hire them. This is <u>very</u> important.

The staff cannot work well together if one staff member leads three people a week to the Lord and the other three staff members average one person a month. We need to train and encourage all the staff to reach out to the lost.

Criminal background and credit checks are essential. Find out from your denomination headquarters about staff people that are doing a very good job in your state (this also helps if you are looking for a pastor). Talk with the previous church secretary about the person you are considering. Get the names and telephone numbers of former secretaries or other church staff members that have previously served with the person you are considering. You will get the best information from staff people that worked with your prospect and then moved on. You want to hear from these people about the prospect's strengths and weaknesses. Call the person's last church and talk with all staff people who have been there during those years your prospect served. Call some of the deacons or lay leaders that know your prospect well.

This will take a lot of work, but it is worth it. You will know before your new staff member arrives what his or her strengths and weaknesses are. You will have the real picture.

When you arrive at a new church, spend a lot of time visiting all your new member prospects and a lot of time getting to know your staff. Give each staff member a list of five things you want them to excel at over the coming months. Tell them you will want to talk with them about the five things every six months. You also want them to keep a list of all the people they have led to Christ and the date that happened.

I took staff people and their spouses out to lunch once a year. I also complimented the staff member in front of the spouse during the lunch. I complimented staff people during our worship services if they had done a great job on something. I promoted great staff by pushing our finance committee to give them a raise.

Have staff meetings every week for an hour. Hit the high spots and let everyone know where we are going in worship, activities, in long-range goals, and what small groups were growing and in what area of the church we need to give more prayer and help.

A lot of church problems can come from confidentiality issues with church staff members. A senior pastor has to take a stand on certain things. However, when a staff member makes a moral mistake, <u>the pastor should not announce that to the church</u>. There are visitors at your church each week. They come to be strengthened in their faith, to make a friend or two, and to enjoy worshiping together with other Christians. People love to see victories for Christ and for their church. They do not want to leave the Sunday service hearing about a moral failure and thinking about the children and teenagers being disappointed. The pastor must lead the service in a positive and uplifting way. His prayers and sermons set the tone for the church.

Years ago, one of the staff members in a large church I was pastoring told the wife of one of our members that he loved her, and that if she would leave her husband, he would leave his wife and they could be together. The wife was not interested in this at all and told one of our other staff, who then told me. As soon as I heard about this, I dealt with it immediately. I went to him and asked if what I heard was true. He said it was. I said, "There is a line and you have stepped over it. I am not going to fire you today, but if you don't write a letter of resignation and give it to me today, I am going to tell all of this to our personnel committee; and they will fire you."

He wrote a generic resignation letter and it was read to our church family at our next service. I didn't say why he was resigning or that we were sorry to see him go.

Within three days, a small group of people sided with the staff member and blamed everything on the woman. I met with the people who were angry with me as well as the other staff who had witnessed his confession to me. The small group left the church. I moved on. I never talked about it and if anyone asked me about it, I referred it to our personnel committee. We hired a new staff member in his position and the church continued to grow.

I also had a staff member who was having an affair with another person on staff. The woman came to my office one day and told me what was happening and that she wanted to stop the affair. She told me this in confidence therefore I could not speak to the other staff member who wanted to continue the affair. I stopped complimenting him (Since I have made the sincere complimenting of staff an integral part of my ministry, this was an obvious change in our working relationship). I asked him if there was anything we needed to pray about together. He resigned at the next service.

I played a lot of sports in high school. To be successful, you don't dwell on the last play; you focus on the next one. As a pastor, deal with the issue, turn it over to Jesus, and move on.

Chapter 7
How To Develop A Sermon

Every sermon should begin with something really interesting. A great joke, a great story, an illustration would be good. Try to make whichever one of these you use to tie in somehow to the sermon. If your first three minutes are bad, you have completely lost 50% of the people.

My seminary preaching professor said we should aim for three points. <u>Each point</u> should be explained, illustrated, and applied. Each point should be related to your scripture. This is the heart of good preaching.

The worst thing someone can say about your sermon is that they never got the point you were trying to make. Advertisers tell us you have to hear something eight times for it to really register in your brain. You want to make your point numerous times, not just in the last line of your sermon.

I preach about stewardship or giving twice a year. I tell people they should tithe to their local church. If you preach about tithing a lot, the people will turn you off and will complain that all you care about is money. You can talk about giving in your bulletin or in emails, but I wouldn't preach about it a lot. In your two sermons about giving, remind people that they will be blessed by God for doing it. Make that a strong point in your two stewardship sermons.

Rather than specifically endorsing or dismissing a political party or politician, I address issues and philosophies that influence our society and government going the wrong way. I preach against socialism and all the welfare programs. I talk about our debt being a horrible thing our children will have to pay. I mention supporting pregnancy care centers and the Baptist Children's Home.

Hopefully, you either have or have access to at least two good commentary sets. You should always read the explanation section of your commentaries to make sure you do not have any theological errors in your train of thought for your sermon. Sometimes you might find a good illustration or better wording for the point you are trying to make.

As you prepare and develop your sermon, make sure it is not too long or too short. If you are on radio or television, twenty-five minutes is your best time allotment. Many preachers preach their sermon and then they re-preach it. People will grow weary of that. Frankly, I believe twenty-five minutes is about right for all sermons. Remember that society's attention span is getting shorter not longer, and that you don't have preach the whole Bible in one sermon. I worked with a Godly education minister named Oscar Calhoun. He said, "I never heard a short talk I didn't like". I have always remembered that. If you are having the Lord's Supper or many baptisms, of course you would need to make your sermon shorter.

I believe you should preach sermons about issues that are headlines in the news. People would like to hear a Christian perspective on current issues. They want to hear what the Bible says about theological and moral and ethical issues on the national and world stage. Many lost people think that the Bible just has old answers to old problems. Ministers need to frame current problems in such a way that all people understand that God has an answer for the troubles we face today.

In order to be well-prepared, you should speak your sermon out loud at least three times before you preach it. Sometimes an adjective or adverb needs to be changed so that vocally you can give the correct emphasis. Speak clearly, don't race through it, and focus on what is helpful. Don't make sarcastic, snide, or otherwise defensive remarks about some recent event that has happened to you with staff or church members. You make yourself look small and it is not helpful.

You ought to keep all your sermons. I write all of mine down word for word. I mark good illustrations so I can find them easily if I want to use that illustration again.

Remember, as you preach you are God's spokesman. There ought to be a dignity about the preaching of the Word of God.

Chapter 8
Where To Get Illustrations

When I was in seminary, I gathered up copies of all the chapel speaker's sermons. I had hundreds of them. I subscribed to a newsletter that a famous preacher put out that included four sermons per month and about twenty good illustrations in each copy. I got on the mailing list of some pastors that would send you a written copy of their Sunday morning sermons for free. I bought sermon books that included hundreds of illustrations. I listened to preachers on TV and wrote down illustrations I liked.

Now with the internet it is a whole new ballgame. You can find thousands of sermons and illustrations for free anytime you want them. The hard thing, of course, is to fit great illustrations to your sermons. If you will take the time to do this, you will have hundreds of great sermons. Though this is a great way to get ideas, it is important that you don't preach another minister's sermons however they are obtained.

I check on the news every day. There are many great illustrations there. I see nothing wrong with telling personal stories. I have people in my church give me copies of jokes they have heard. Never, never tell an off-color joke you have cleaned up! Someone in the audience will have heard the original version and it will scare them to death for fear of what you might say! If you have a great start to your sermon and a great finish, and the middle part is not too long, you have a great sermon.

Chapter 9
What To Say At A Funeral

What to say at a funeral begins to develop way before the person dies. Whenever I am visiting with someone who is critically ill and has a small chance of recovering, I talk with the family about writing down important events and involvements in the dying person's life. I ask them to highlight places where they have served in the church, when they were saved, and how long they have been a member of the church. I always mention these things in the funeral.

It is important to visit with the dying person and to find out what was really important in his/her life. I try to notice if they have a Bible close to their bed. I ask them what their favorite verse is. All of these things can be used in the funeral sermon and it helps to personalize the service.

When I was growing up, my parents never took me to a funeral. I went to college without ever being at a funeral. My freshman year at Baylor, I got serious about trying to be the pastor of a church. I felt God leading me in that direction. The White Mound Baptist Church, just 25 miles from Waco, Texas, called me to be their pastor. I was so excited about it. I still had never been to a funeral. After I had been at the church for four months, a man died that I had never met and that was not a member of our church. Our church was the only church in that town. The family asked me to do the funeral.

I thought I would call the funeral home that handled all the funerals in that area and get someone to help me to know how to lead a funeral service. One of the men that worked there was very nice and told me about what went on at a funeral. He made some suggestions about the Scriptures I should use.

I went to the home where the deceased had lived. There were about ten people there and they were glad to see me. I told them I would do the funeral service. I didn't tell them that I had never been to a funeral. I asked them what the man died from. Some of them looked at the floor and the rest of them looked at the ceiling. Not one of them said a word. I wondered what was going on. One man offered me a coke. I drank it and asked the man that gave me the coke what the man had died from. He led me over to the corner of the room, away from anyone else. He said the man had died in bed with a woman that was not his wife.

The funeral was very short and everyone was glad when it was over, particularly me. I visited the funeral home for the next three of four funerals and learned how different ministers conducted a funeral. The Lord was gracious and helped me learn many things during my first year in ministry. These were meaningful ministerial moments.

I worked in a funeral home while in seminary and I heard hundreds and hundreds of funeral sermons. I took notes. I also drove families from their homes to the church or from their homes to the funeral home. I then would drive them from the service back to their homes. On the way back home, the families would talk about the funeral service, and they would mention what they liked and didn't like. I listened and took notes.

Families like to hear, obviously, the good points about the deceased. If you know the deceased was not a nice person and had many failings in their life, I say this, "Mr. Jones had some difficult times and situations in life. He did some wonderful things and he had some failures in his life, like all of us do." If you don't say something like that, the people at the funeral will think you are less than an honest person.

Families do not want to find out at the funeral service that you are a great Bible scholar. It is not the time for an in-depth Bible study. It is the time for you to remember the deceased, to point out the good things in their life, to assure the family that the deceased is in a better place, and to mention that family and friends can see the deceased person again if they are Christians (1 Corinthians 13:12).

If the deceased was not a Christian to the best of your knowledge, I would not try to preach them into heaven. In that case, I usually read the 23rd Psalm and apply the passage to the people in attendance. I speak about the grace of God that we have studied about in Sunday School and church all of our lives is now available to them. Mention the Lord's presence is with them that day and for the days that are just ahead.

The worst funerals I have attended are the ones where there are five preachers and four music specials. In that case, usually the pastor is the last speaker; and by that time, everyone is ready for it to be over. The pastor of the church should make sure that everyone on the platform knows about how long they should speak. If the person speaking doesn't quit when they are supposed to, I will say, "Thank you, brother," as I rise from my seat.

Another terrible thing that happens is when everyone is invited to speak, and people get up and say inappropriate things. I would work with the family beforehand to make sure this does not happen. It's always better to let the professionals do it.

The funeral sermon should be related to the deceased a number of times. If the family wants you to present the Gospel, by all means do it. I would introduce it by saying, "The Jones family wanted me to make sure that everyone here today knows how to be a Christian. I know you would like to visit again with Mr. Jones; this is how you can do it." A funeral service is not purposed to be a revival service....that comes later.

The funeral sermon should not be over twenty-five minutes long. If there is a place for any appropriate humor, I would use it. Especially if it is related to the deceased, but I would get the family's blessing.

Below I have listed a few things that I have used hundreds of times.

- There is a democracy about death—it comes to all of us.
- What he/she has seen by faith, he/she has now seen by sight.
- John 11:25 says we will never die. Where will you spend eternity?
- In heaven there is no more crying, no more sighing, and no more dying.

Chapter 10
How To Show Love For The People

Some preachers stay in a back room somewhere and they walk out when they know it is time to be on the platform. After the service is over, they quickly go to the back room somewhere. That performance mentality separates you from the people.

I am always the first person in the worship center before the service. I always tried to meet as many people as possible, especially those who had been out sick or those that had been away on a vacation. Of course, the visitors are of special importance. I would write down the prospect's names and something about them that I could bring up when we talked again or when I visited them at home. People love to be remembered.

Train your members to greet those whom they do not know and say, "We are going out to lunch after the service and we would love to have you meet us there." This is really impressive to first-time visitors.

After the service is over, I stood at the back door and visited with as many people as possible. If your church gives you an allowance to take people out to eat, I would do it every Sunday. The prospects you take out would never forget it and would feel honored by you.

Of course, hospital visitation is extremely important. Have your youth minister visit all the children in the hospital and your senior adult minister visit all of the seniors, and the minister of music should tend to the choir members and others in music ministry.

A phone call after they leave the hospital is <u>very</u> important. Call everyone that has had surgery.

I have always tried to go to all the small group, choir, and deacon parties. Remembering hundreds or thousands of names is very difficult but going to group meetings helps. The people in your church <u>love</u> your attention. Go to women's group meetings and mission group meetings. You don't have to stay, but it is great to show up and shake hands. Let them know that you care about them and what ministry they are involved in. Make friends with your people. You grow as a person, as a Christian, and as a pastor as you develop friendships with church members.

Show gratitude. Yes, the members are supposed to attend worship, tithe, give, work in ministry, etc. However, everyone needs affirmation. When you tell them how much you appreciate what they are doing, you show love.

When not sure how to decide in a situation between judgement and grace, ere on the side of grace. Many preachers especially when starting out, succumb to insecurity and become defensive, telling people off during a sermon or face to face because of some hurt the pastor has experienced or imagined. You appear small, judgmental, and unloving. It's not effective in the long run and can hurt your ministry by making everything about you. As a leader you need to rise above the day-to-day pettiness and lead. Bossiness and authoritarianism does not inspire or encourage your people. This will also help your staff as they see you as a mature Christian. This will promote church wide unity rather than a staff verses membership mentality. It will help the staff to model your behavior, love the church members, and not focus on the insignificant. Unity does not mean expecting complete agreement on everything you want to do. A great leader has the ability to value other people's opinions and listen to other people's perspectives.

Once a year, lead a group on a trip somewhere. You get to know those people that go on the trip with you, and it gives you a break from your daily difficult schedule. It is a good thing for everyone, and those who go along will tell all the folks back home what a wonderful time they had with you.

Chapter 11
How To Motivate Sunday Small Groups

Get the records of past attendance in each of the groups. If a class is going down in attendance, you need to take action. If you have a Minister of Education, get him and all of the small group members and have a frank conversation with them. You go as well. Start the meeting by saying something like this (the Minister of Education speaking): "We have noticed that your attendance has gone down this past year. We all want to see that changed. We want to go around the room and listen to each of you give ideas about how we could build up your class. Take notes on what each person says. Put all of the ideas on a sheet of paper, including ideas from you and the Minister of Education.

Sometimes the time for prayer requests in Sunday School groups lasts way too long. Some people in the class are already depressed and a half hour of sad stories does not help. Sometimes one person will talk too long about his or her needs or problems in the family. Make it a rule in the class that no one can talk over two minutes. If someone has a terrible smell about them, that needs to be addressed privately.

Have a high attendance day each year and get each class to set an attendance goal. Take four weeks to build up to the high attendance day. The first Sunday have your class go out to eat together. When someone says the blessing, have them say in the prayer, "Lord, please help us to each bring a guest on high attendance day." On the second Sunday, have each class member mention the name of the person they are trying to get there for the high attendance Sunday. On the third Sunday, mention that you are going to give a present to the person who brings the most guests. Get a nice present, a restaurant gift card. On that high attendance day, celebrate what God has done. If that doesn't help, you need to change leaders in the class.

Years ago, when I was leading a single adult ministry in a large church, there were some people that didn't think we were "feeding the people. They told me that their class was too superficial. They complained that their teacher was not able to do an in-depth class.

Another one of our classes went from ten to a hundred and ten in six months. Many people were being saved and many were joining the church. Three or four people in that class came to me and said they thought their class was great for meeting people and making friends, but not great for growing spiritually.

I decided to enlist five people that were not happy from both of those classes and put them together in a new class. I asked a man that had joined our church that was single and was a seminary graduate to teach that new class. I told him I wanted the class to be scholarly and in depth. I asked him to give people in the class homework and to tackle theological issues.

The next week I announced in our opening assembly to all of the people that we were starting a new class that would be an in-depth class with very serious Bible study. When the open assembly was over, about ten people came up to me and said they were so happy to hear about the new class. Some of those that had been complaining for over a year about our classes being superficial were thrilled to death. One lady said, "Thank God, we are finally going to have an in-depth class."

The next Sunday we started the new class and twenty-five people came. After the class was over, I saw a few of the people from the class in the hall and I asked them how the class was going. They all said it was great. I asked if they had gone deeper. They all smiled and said yes. In the next few weeks, a few more people joined that class. However, as the months went by, the class started to get smaller. I felt like I had done everything I could do. After about six months, the class had four people in it. All of our other classes were growing. I realized that those people in the small class were not going to be happy.

People in ministry should try to meet every single need they can. However, accept the fact that some people are just not going to be satisfied. Don't let that fact depress you and cause you to resign.

Chapter 12
How To Make A Hospital Visit

Over the years, I have had many people tell me after the service, "Pastor, did you know that Mr. Jones is in the hospital? As I left church, I would drive by the hospital to check on Mr. Jones. When I went in, the lady at the information desk said there was no one there by that name. I found out later I had been given the name of the wrong hospital or that that person went home three hours earlier. I am so thankful for cell phones. I always call and find out for sure that our members are at a certain hospital; and they have not been dismissed yet. This will save you a lot of time and gas.

Wash your hands before you go into hospital rooms. You don't want to carry in germs from something you have touched (doors or elevators, or people you have seen and shaken hands with, or from other patients). Remember to wash your hands again before you leave the hospital.

Figure out the best place for you to be so patients can see you. If the patient is flat on their back, stand over them beside their bed. If they have their head elevated in their bed, move your chair to where they can see you.

Shortly after entering the hospital room, say hello to all the other people in the room. Ask if they are relatives or friends of the patient. Ask where they are from and how long they will be in town. Get their phone numbers because you might need to call them at a later time. Tell all of those visiting in the room your phone number. Tell them you love the patient, and you want to be updated on the patient's condition. Try to build a relationship with family members. This procedure will give you an opportunity to minister to the patient and to the family. Leave one of your cards in an obvious place in the room. Focus on positive things the family or friends say. Repeat those things in your prayer just before you leave the room. If the patient is in intensive care, you will not know how long they will be there. Call them the next day to learn about their progress.

Make sure the family and friends know that you and the whole church will be praying for the patient. Make sure the patient knows that God is with them and that God loves them.

Before leaving, ask the patient and the family if there is anything you can do for them. Maybe they will want some water or to see a nurse. Show them the button that they need to press to ask for help from a nurse. I would push the button then, and if there is no response, I go out in the hall and find a nurse and ask them to visit the room of your patient.

Be sure you thank the family and friends for their presence and their love for the patient. Tell them many patients at the hospital have no visitors and they, of course, get very lonely. Stand beside the patient's bed and pray for them as you are about to leave. Pray for the patient's health and healing, but don't say God will heal them. God might take them home to heaven.

Don't stay too long. When I was a freshman at Baylor University, I started pastoring a small country church when I was 19. After I had been there for a month, our pianist (who was the only piano player at the church) had serious surgery at the closest hospital. She was not only the church pianist, but one of the main leaders in the church. I wanted to do a great job as her pastor, so I arrived at the hospital before she went in for her surgery and had prayer with her. I went to the waiting room and stayed for about three hours. When they took her to her room, I was there waiting for her to arrive. I felt like I was doing a great job as her pastor. I stayed for about four hours in her small room with her. We talked some and I studied some for my classes the next day. When they brought her supper, I felt like I had done a superior job staying with her the whole time, and I could now leave after all I had done.

She was in the hospital for two days and then went home. When I saw her at church, I went over and hugged her, and she said she wanted to talk with me for a few moments. We went into a small, empty classroom and sat down.

She said, "Pastor, I really appreciate you being at the hospital early and staying with me all day, but I do want to mention to you that people in the hospital sometimes need to pass some gas. It is very difficult to do that if your pastor is six feet away. You might want to think about staying in a hospital room with a patient for about fifteen minutes."

I learned a lot that day. She was a wonderful person. If a patient says they are tired, you need to leave quickly. Call them later in the day. Be <u>very</u> sensitive to the patient. Call them the next day and check on them. Say, "God bless you in Jesus' name."

Always stay in touch with the church office. Give them and all of the other ministers the latest word on the patient. If you don't have staff hospital visits on a rotating basis, encourage them to visit but on different days. Avoid duplicate visits on the same day.

Chapter 13

How To Reach Out To Single Adults

> ## Meet 500 Singles for Free
> (Insert photo of eclectic group of attractive people)
>
> Cost to you is two hours on Sunday morning. This is a family setting where you don't have to buy drinks or be the best dancer in town. This is a place where there is love and acceptance in a positive Christian atmosphere. If you haven't been to church in 5 or 10 years you owe it to yourself to give it a try. Call John Smith xxx-xxx-xxxx for further information. 500 singles will say hi! If you can't make it Sunday, each Thursday night at 8:00 there is a casual adult Bible Study for local singles. *Include name of church and address.*

This is similar to the actual advertising materials I used when I was the single adult pastor in Dallas at Northway Baptist Church. When I left the church to pastor a church in Arizona, we had over 900 singles.

A little lady named Siri who lives in my iPhone said that there are 252 million adults in America. She also said that 129 million people were married. That would leave 123 million singles. I have not been able to find out how many people live together without being married.

As the years go by, for young and middle-aged adults cohabitation is up and marriage is down. Among those ages 18-24 cohabitation is now more prevalent than living with a spouse. In 2018, 15 percent of young adults ages 25-34 lived with an unmarried partner, up from 12 percent ten years prior. Today, 30 percent of young adults ages 18-34 are married, but 40 years ago, in 1978, 59 percent (nearly double) of young adults were married. All of these numbers mean that churches should strive to reach single adults for the Lord. The pastor and church leaders should all realize that single adults make up a huge percentage of the population of America. If we are going to fulfill the Great Commission, we <u>have to</u> reach single adults.

Today when you go out on visitation from your church, you need to have a few sentences in your mind to say when you find out that the people you are visiting are living together, but not married. The "you are going to hell" line has never welcomed a sinner to the family of God. You have to remember, you are not going to make everyone perfect on your first visit. You need to make a friend with one or, hopefully, both of them as you visit.

In the early 1980's, I was the single adult minister at Northway Baptist Church in Dallas. We had 100 singles enrolled. I left four years later, and we had over 900 enrolled. We had over 500 in attendance on Sunday mornings. I didn't have the slightest idea what I was doing, but I was willing to work hard and try a lot of different things. Some of those things worked.

People who have just divorced or experience the death of a mate usually stay home for a couple of weeks crying or drinking. They begin to feel alone after these horrible events in their lives. They might have a few friends that are single adults. If those singles reach out to this person who is suddenly alone, they can be a great help to their newly single friend.

I pleaded with all our singles to reach out to men or women that are suddenly single. Some that they invited came to our mass meeting on Sunday morning. They were always surprised at this large gathering. Their thought process said that they had to adjust to their new life. Many of the new visitors decided on that first Sunday to get involved with these people they did not know.

I started the singles group eating lunch every Sunday in some restaurant close by and we always announced where we were going. I trained the group to wait at the front door so we could all go in together. When we started having over 100 for Sunday lunch, it became a great witness for our church, and we would always look for people sitting alone. Some of our group would go and sit all around the person. Of course, that person would ask someone seated around them who we were. Our singles would immediately say, "We are the single adults from Northway Baptist Church." Many of those people would come and visit the following Sunday. Pizza places where there were long tables made it perfect for us to sit all around people sitting alone.

On Thursday nights each week we would advertise a Bible study for singles. Many visitors would come. I would have a good singer to start the evening. Then I would say, "Please meet the person in front of you and the person behind you." When they finished that, I would say meet the people that are to your right and left. We had coffee and cokes out before anyone arrived.

I would do a Bible study that <u>related</u> to singles. I added humor and kept it short. I told funny stories about singles. Since I was single, I made jokes about myself.

When I finished teaching, I said, "Hang around, meet everyone in the room." That is why they came. They wanted to meet other singles. Don't talk about the Sea of Galilee. No one cares about that. Thursday nights were a great success.

There were in Dallas, at that time, huge complexes of apartments filled with singles. Everyone knew hundreds and hundreds of singles lived in that area. We decided we were going to reach those singles for the Lord. On over 400 apartment doors we taped a little note telling when and where the Bible study would be. One of our single church members lived in that complex, and so we said that's where the study would be. The first week we had one single lady come. We thought, "Well, let's try again." We went to every door and left a taped message for every single. The second week we had no visitors. That was the end of that effort.

We trained our singles to notice people sitting alone in a worship service and they were able to give them a rundown on who we were and what we did. Some of our leaders would make sure the people were invited to our singles class and they were told all about our church.

Once every other month we would go out for "A Night of Fine Dining." We would meet at the church at a certain time and carpool to the restaurant. We once again would walk in together and sit around people eating alone. We had many people visit our church because so many people would reach out to them. The "Night of Fine Dining" restaurants were a bit more pricey. We had to have people sign up. For many people this would be the nicest thing they did all year. Many of our ladies wanted to go to a nice restaurant so they could dress up in their nice clothes.

Once a year we would go to some beach or some nice place in the mountains. We would rent rooms for two or three nights. We also went skiing or mountain climbing or to Europe or Hawaii. There were some people that were ready to go no matter how far away we went. All of these outings brought in singles from all over Dallas. Many grew spiritually and began to take leadership positions in our ministry.

Our attitude was always very positive. We trained our people not to make someone feel guilty if they could not go to some event. There would always be many more events.

We had special classes for single parents and retreats for them with their children.

Many churches at that time did not want singles in their church. They felt like they didn't have time for these singles. At those churches, singles would come and go. Very few joined or stayed very long. They wanted to be at a church that would welcome and love them.

Many people thought that the singles were immoral, and they didn't want that influence in their church. Many wives in the church didn't feel like these single women visitors would stay away from their husbands. Some of the wives in the churches were actually rude to the single ladies. Many of those singles ended up at our church.

Many singles are abrupt or hostile because of desertion or death of their mate. Mature Christians need to help the singles that have had horrific deaths or divorces in their marriages. Many of these singles are strong Christians but are just temporarily in a <u>very</u> difficult time in their lives.

Many people in the Dallas church where I served as the singles minister really resented what I was doing in building up the singles group. Some told me I was running a meat market where singles came to find someone to sleep with. I don't know what the exact percentage was, but some of the singles did come to find someone to sleep with. When someone would say that to me, I would say in response, "Have you noticed how many each week came forward to make a public profession of their faith in Jesus?" I would tell them how many we had baptized that year. The numbers were significant. We had over 200 take a stand for Jesus and become active in the church each year. There were also hundreds of visitors each month.

Toward the end of my ministry at Northway Baptist Church the singles outnumbered the married people in the church. That horrified some of the leaders. They didn't want their church to become known as a single adult church. One of the leaders of the church came to me one day and said, "Ron, we are not going to give you any more rooms for Bible study or any more money in the church budget."

I mentioned to him he ought to check out the offerings given by the singles. I encouraged the singles to give their offerings during Bible study. Their giving was significant. I found out the exact amount the singles gave each week and told him that amount. He was very surprised. I asked him then if he and his wife were planning to die at the same time. He said, "Probably not."

I said, "Wouldn't it be nice if there was a Bible study class already functioning that was designated for people that had lost their mate?" I had trained a group of people in that class to reach out to those in the church who had just lost their mate. Everyone who went into that class was received well and really helped by the people who had suffered that loss in their lives as well. The class talked about growing through grief about every third month. That class had a great strong testimony to the strength of the program.

He looked at me and said, "Well, I guess my wife will go in that class." I replied, "You know, all souls are of equal value. These singles want to go to heaven just like the married people do." He then turned and walked away. The next day I began looking for another church.

I learned a lot about what singles were looking for in that church. I was trying very hard to build up our singles group. I was very disappointed when a couple announced that they were going to get married because that meant that those two would be leaving us. Of course, I was happy for them, but I would miss them being with us.

Once, three weeks in a row, I made the announcement that two in our group were getting married. On the fourth week, we had more visitors than usual. I asked the newcomers what brought then to our church. Almost all of them said, "We heard a lot of folks were getting married here, so we wanted to come and find out what was going on." From then on, I was happy to announce engagements. The word really got around about hundreds of marriages taking place at Northway.

When singles join the church, many of them have one or two or three children. This, or course, builds up the children's ministry and the middle school ministry. Many singles have relatives in the area, and they will begin to visit and join as well. Senior adult singles will come and visit as well. Basically, the single adult ministry will be a blessing to all the age groups in the church.

It is important that the senior pastor has the right perspective on single adults. He or she needs to preach a sermon each year, encouraging singles to join the church family. The senior pastor also needs to attend some of the activities of the singles during the year. The senior pastor <u>has</u> to be on board with the singles ministry.

Some people have asked me, "How do you have a good climate for single adult ministry?" Let me list a few things.

- Do not change workers every year. Compliment every worker who is doing a good job. Ask the best leaders to your house for dinner, and while they are there help them to see your vision about how the singles' ministry can grow. Get suggestions from them on how your group can grow. Talk about the percentage of singles in your area.
- Have workers that can affirm and challenge singles to grow spiritually. Don't let anyone become a teacher until you have asked them to sub a few times in different classes. Get feedback from those classes before you ask them to teach a class.
- Do not get negative legalists in this area. If, for instance, a person you are considering for a leadership position said, "No Christian would dance or drink wine." Since Jesus made wine and spiritual leaders in the Bible danced before the Lord, you might want to rethink that person for certain positions. You always need greeters and people to make the coffee.

- Realize that you are ministering in an area where the three most stressful things in life may have occurred (death of a mate, divorce, getting fired).
- Realize the Lord is using you to meet spiritual needs. If you have been divorced or your mate had died, you can say some helpful things to people that are just entering those hurtful situations. Don't try to become a psychologist or psychiatrist. If the person needs that kind of help, be sure to recommend someone that has had that training.

People have asked me, "What kind of structure do you set up for singles?" Let me list the plan of action and the people that are needed to make the system work.

Always have your leaders arrive fifteen minutes early. The greeters, of course, need to be there early. I always tried to enlist extroverted people for that job. Have the chairs arranged in a semi-circle facing the microphone. If you can, always have coffee and donuts and orange juice. Start on time with all the singles meeting together. You want to win the psychological battle of having a large crowd together. (This group is not for college and career students.)

If you just have 5 or 10 singles, after they are greeted send them to the classroom where they will sit down with the class leaders. If the group is large, over 50, start with a positive song, not "Precious Memories." If the music is bad, don't have any music. Don't introduce visitors in the large group, introduce them in the classroom.

Be sure to introduce the visitors the same way each week. Ask them where they were born. Ask them what they do. Do not ask them where they work. If they say they work at the airport don't ask them if they are a pilot. Their job might be to clean up the planes in between flights. Your enlisted leaders should be very positive people who want every visitor to feel at home.

Do not let unstable people or negative people dominate the hour. I once had a teacher come to me and say, "I have a fellow in my class that won't quit interrupting me. He is ruining our class and I can't get him to stop talking." I asked if I could teach for him the next Sunday. He said, "I would be thrilled if you teach."

I started teaching and a man I didn't know rudely interrupted. I listened for about two minutes, and then I interrupted him. I taught for about four minutes, and he interrupted me again. I said, "We want to hear from everyone in our class and we have heard from you." He didn't interrupt me again. When the class was over, I walked over to him and said, "You have been repeatedly interrupting the teacher of this class and today you interrupted me twice. You are going to have to stop that. I believe you could make more friends and help the class to grow if you just maintained silence for three to four weeks." I asked the teacher the next week if the interrupter interrupted the class. The teacher said, "No, and the man was not a problem again." A couple months later, this same guy that had been interrupting came up to me and said, "You know, when you told me that I had to be quiet, I wanted to punch you in the face. But now I want to thank you. After three or four weeks, the teacher actually asked for my opinion. Then a few of the class members asked me to go to lunch. I didn't realize that my talking all the time was such a turn off. You really helped me."

The teacher should conclude the Bible study each week with a question time. The questions can be about the lesson or other issues that need clarification.

Put the chairs in a circle if possible. Remember the church service is for praise and worship. During Bible study time you share with others and get to know each other in addition to explaining God's Word.

The most important five minutes on Sunday morning are between Bible study and worship. Train your leaders to take the visitors to worship with them. Have at least ten leaders in each class from the day it starts.

Never ask <u>guests</u> to read the Bible or give a testimony. Don't put your regular class members on the spot, either. You might embarrass someone by making them feel inadequate if they don't know the answer or if they are poor readers. Instead, ask a question to the whole group and pause long enough for people to get their thoughts together and answer. To break up the lesson, ask the group for a volunteer to read the next set of scripture verses. Find out from your class members who is comfortable praying out loud before you call on an individual to pray.

The ten leaders and their responsibilities are as follows:

1. *Director*. The Director is enlisted by the singles minister. The director should make sure the class has a monthly class meeting. All class leaders should be at this meeting. The discussion should relate to progress in spirit and planning of the class. Class difficulties should be worked out at the class meeting, never on Sunday morning. If any class leader is not doing their job, the director is responsible for retraining or removing the person. The director (perhaps a husband-and-wife team) enlists and trains people for every job in the class except that of teacher. The director needs to talk with all of the workers regularly. In a growing singles ministry, you will have exceptional Christian singles joining weekly. They should be trained and put to work quickly.

2. *Teacher*. The teacher is enlisted by the singles minister. This person should meet every visitor in the class each week. They should also call every visitor each week to welcome them to the class. Be sure to arrive early and stay at least 10 minutes after class to answer any questions class members want to ask. Remember there are people in every class with very little religious training. In every class there are also some people that are spiritually mature. In each lesson there should be something for both groups. Deal with every question seriously. Do not let class members laugh at one another. Do not begin to teach until every class member has access to a Bible or lesson

book with the Scripture in it. Try to make the Biblical material relate to single adults today. Do not just teach a history lesson about some biblical mountain. There should be three parts of every major point you present: explain the Scripture, illustrate the Scripture, and apply the Scripture.

3. *Class President*. This person starts every class with introduction of guests and announcements about class and division activities. This should be an extroverted, warm person.

4. *Class Vice-President*. This person takes over when the class president is absent. The vice-president should make sure there is a calendar of all activities on the wall of the classroom.

5. *Planning Coordinator*. This person is responsible for planning and coordinating all of the activities of the class. This person makes sure that everyone has the details of each event.

6. *Outreach Leader*. This person makes sure that every class visitor is visited every week. This person goes visiting and trains the person that goes with them on how to lead someone to Christ.

7. *In-reach Leader*. This person checks on everyone that misses the class for two weeks in a row. If they miss three weeks in a row, they give the absentee's name to the teacher to contact as well.

8. *Mission Coordinator*. This person plans three or four one-day mission projects each year. They work in conjunction with other mission coordinators in other classes. They can do things like paint the inside or the

outside of a poor person's house. They could trim trees or build a ramp in the front of the person's house to help someone in a wheelchair. The projects should be for one day, not a week.

9. <u>*Class Secretary*</u>. This person keeps all class and financial records. They are in charge of sending cards, texts, and emails to those class members who are very ill.

10. <u>*Other Class Leaders*</u>. These people might be greeters, someone to make coffee, someone to bring orange juice, someone to bring donuts. As people are faithful in these jobs, they are given jobs with more responsibility.

People from other churches across the country have asked me what type of leaders I try to enlist. Let me mention a few of the things I looked for.

- Someone that understands "grace" theologically. Jesus denounced the legalists, the Pharisees, and all of those today who think they are much more spiritual than anyone else. Remember, grace is the unmerited favor of God.
- Someone who believes God's Word. The Bible is our handbook, our marching orders, and our authority. Many singles find that their lives are in chaos. Leaders with singles should know the Scripture in order to help singles back to a life of significance and meaning.

- Someone who is positive and assertive. Depressed people need help, not a leadership position. Negative people need to understand that Jesus brought an abundant life. We have a lot to be positive about: a risen Lord, a great church, and the good news of the Gospel. When we have such a great message, it is easy to aggressively share it.
- Someone who can forgive. We continuously need to pray that God will make us forgiving people. "Vengeance is mine" (said the Lord) Deuteronomy 32:35. Sometimes we try to help God "get" someone. It is much better to forgive.
- People that don't have to tell everything they know about everybody we know.

General Concepts

- If someone has a questionable reputation, do not let them lead anything.
- Have consistent people in ministry. You cannot build a strong Christian program on secular, flighty people.
- Keep ministry plans simple and go over them time and time again. Make people understand the big picture.
- Some singles want to be in a martyr's club. Do not put those people in any leadership position.
- Make sure visitors feel accepted. If they do not, find out why. Negative, critical people will kill your group.

- Have the leaders over to your house. Make them feel like they are in the inner circle. Hug them. Love them. Give yourself to them.
- Make sure there are some Type A personalities in each singles class. They are workaholics and they will build the class if you will train them.
- Take ideas that are working in one class and share them with all the other classes.
- Colossians 2:10 says that we find our completeness in Jesus Christ. You do not have to be married to be complete. Neither our Lord nor Paul were married.
- Believe I John 1:9, "If we confess our sins, He is faithful and just to forgive us our sins, and to cleanse us from all unrighteousness." There is **not** an asterisk beside that verse and at the bottom of the page that says, "except for divorce".
- Give singles meaningful jobs in the church; do not just put them on the parking committee.
- Have specialized training for singles that have been divorced to work with newly divorced singles. Have a special group for those that have suffered the death of a mate, money problems, time management, etc.
- Singles will make short-term commitments to ministry tasks. Do not ask people to serve some way like every Monday night forever.
- If possible, build an athletic program (softball league or tennis ladder or golf tournaments). If your city has an athletic program, try to involve your

singles in that. It can be a great witness and a way to reach out to others.

• You need to have some spiritual leadership at all social events. Sometimes a group can go the wrong way in events like retreats. Leadership can help the direction of group events if there are no ministers present.

• Make sure singles working in other divisions of the church are informed monthly of all single events.

• Every single adult visitor should have a visit in their home by two singles the week they visit a Bible study event.

• Every visitor should receive a letter from the church the week they visit. You want the visitor to see the full program of the church.

• Have most of your fellowships in homes, not at the church.

• Have cafeteria style programming. Do not make people feel guilty if they don't go to everything.

• I believe twenty to thirty in attendance is the perfect size for a single adult class.

• Try to build a single adult ensemble and then try to build a single adult choir.

• Singles need to help others rather than focusing just on their own problems. Get them involved in some mission's program as soon as possible. Some singles will come and need attention and caring immediately. Have the name and phone number of a local

Christian counselor that you can recommend immediately.

- I know everyone would not feel comfortable with this, but I liked introducing new singles to someone in our group. The result was a lot of marriages.

Years ago, I was pastoring a church in Arizona and there was a man in the church named Fred. His wife was very ill when I started there and continued to be very ill while I pastored that church. One day the sad phone call came. Fred's wife died. He called to give me the news and I went to the house to visit with Fred. He came to church the following Sunday, and everyone reached out to him. He continued to be present each Sunday. After six or seven weeks, Fred called me and wanted to come to the church and have a talk with me. We set it up for the next day.

When Fred arrived, he sat down and said, "I want to get married." He said he hated being alone all the time. I asked if he felt like his grieving period was over. I didn't want him to rush into anything, but he was ready to move on. I couldn't slow him down. He said, "Ron, you date all the time (I was single then), how about lining me up with some nice lady? Do you think anyone would want to go out with me?"

I said, "Well, of course, I know some very nice single ladies." Many single ladies in the church had asked me to find them a man. I called one that had asked me four or five times to find her someone. I called Fred and set it up. I asked her to call me after the date and tell me how it went. When she called, she was not happy. She said, "Ron, that was the worst date I have ever had in my life." I asked, "What went wrong?"

She said in the first five minutes he said he was 68 years old, owned his house and car, had a great retirement, was a Christian, and wanted to get married. She said she pulled her chair back and wanted to go home. I called Fred the next morning and set up a meeting with him. I asked him, "How did the date go?" He said, "I don't believe she liked me. Do you know any other single ladies?" I said, "Let's talk a little. How many dates have you had in your life? He said, "Last night was my first one. I started going with my wife in the 6th grade."

I said, "Fred, let me coach you a little on what you say on your next date. Ask her where she is from. Ask if she had any children. Ask her what kind of work she has done. Ask her where she has gone to church. Ask her what states and countries she has visited."

Fred wrote all my suggestions down and then said, "Is there another lady that might go out with me?" I told him there were many wonderful Christian ladies that would love to go out with him. I then asked him some more questions. Fred had a very ugly red, very old sports jacket. He loved it, but it was terrible. I told him that jacket was too formal for a casual date. I said, "Don't wear the jacket." I said, "Don't say you want to get married on the first date." I asked, "Where did you take her to eat?" He told me about a place in town that wasn't very nice. I told him of a nice restaurant near the shopping center. I said, "Take her there." I gave him the name and phone number of another lady that had asked me many times to find her a husband. I called the lady and told her a friend of mine named Fred would be calling her for a date. I told her he had recently lost his wife and he really didn't know how to date. I asked her to be gentle with him.

He called her and set up the date. He didn't wear his ugly red sports jacket. He did take her to the nice restaurant. He went through my talking points and then the conversation slowed down. He decided to say, "I am 68 years old, I own my house and car." He said he had a great retirement and that he was a Christian, and he wanted to get married.

I had asked her to call me after their date and tell me how it went. She called me that night and said, "It was very difficult to continue the conversation with him after he said, "I want to get married." She said she was not going to go out with him again. I called him the next morning and asked him how the date went. He said, "I don't think she liked me." I said, "I have another lady friend that I want you to meet."

I called Mary, whom I had known for a long time. She had given up on men but was certainly open to going on a date again. I gave him her name and number. I warned her of his speech about his house and car being paid off, his great retirement, and that he wanted to get married. She laughed and said, "I can handle that."

They sent up the date and I asked her to call me when she got home. She called late that night and was laughing. She said,

"Ron, he is a very nice Christian man. I have never had a man I had a date with say a blessing. When he said how old he was, I told him how old I was. When he said that his house and car were paid off, I told him my house and car were paid off. When he said he had a great retirement, I told him I had a great retirement. When he said he wanted to get married, I said I wanted to get married. We have another date set up next week."

Mary and Fred started coming to church together, and two months later I did their wedding. They had a wonderful marriage. I so wish dating singles would give each other a chance and not cut it all off in the first ten minutes. The first date that singles have with someone ought to be where they meet at a coffee house, a restaurant or for some activity.

- Introduce singles to other singles if you think they might have a good time together. Don't be apologetic about it. It is much better than them meeting in bars.
- Do not have an all-divorced class. It makes the singles think they have a virus and that you are afraid it is going to spread.
- Remember, only about 7 percent of Americans live in a home where there is a mother and a father and two or more of their children.
- Some people have asked me how to advertise their single adult groups. Use social media and emphasize the words "single adult" and "acceptance." Singles from the secular world are not attracted by the words "Bible study and prayer." If you are short on men,

advertise with the local sports leagues in your area. Blanket mailings to all the zip codes in your area are a very effective methodology. You want to reach the unsaved. **Go after them.**

In Romans 14 and 15, Paul talked about two groups in the Christian community in Rome when he names "the weak and the strong." The strong were ex-idolaters, freshly converted from paganism. The weak were legalists, and, for the most part, Jewish Christians. Paul had a conciliatory attitude toward the weak, not allowing the strong (Gentile Christians) to despise, browbeat, or condemn them.

Paul wanted to enable the Jewish Christians and the Gentile Christians to co-exist amicably in the Christian fellowship. The strong Christians did not follow the Jewish laws and rejoiced in their Christian freedom, as did Paul. Paul made it quite clear that he believed the position of the strong was correct. He basically just wanted all people to trust in Christ and show love and kindness toward each other.

Many ministers and married people today see single adults as transient individuals that you cannot count on to help in the ministry of the church or to stay around for very long. Many single adults that visit our churches are new to how we do things. They are used to wearing shorts and tennis shoes. They like to raise their hands in worship and talk (many times loudly) until the first song begins. Singles love to be welcomed when they walk into church, and it would be <u>great</u> if someone called out to them to come and sit with them. It would be even better if they were invited to go to lunch with some people that they have met at the church. We need to train our church members to do this. Many church members want to sit in the same seats each week with the same people each week. If we are going to double our church, we <u>have to</u> reach out to people.

We need to encourage singles to join the choir and get on various committees. Getting involved in various kinds of missions' work is a great way to help singles feel like a part of the church family.

Paul reached out to everyone. He didn't care about their background. He cared about their relationship to Jesus. That is exactly what we ought to do. Some singles are weak in their faith because when they were divorced, many people pulled away from them. Some singles are angry about the way their small children are treated at church. The methodology that the church has for ministering to small children should be fully explained and the parents should be walked around to observe the layout of the church.

Those that are weak in their faith <u>need</u> attention and love and smiles. Some single adults that visit your church will be strong in their faith, their tithing, and anxious to serve in some way. We need to plug them in <u>quickly</u>. Paul bathed his whole ministry in prayer. We should do that as we try to reach singles for Christ.

Chapter 14

How To Show Love To Senior Adults

As I grew older, I retired at 65 years of age. The church was very nice and gave me $10,000 as a gift. I took my wife, Cindy, to Hawaii for two weeks and we had a wonderful time. When we got back home, it took me about three days to get anxious. I didn't have anything I had to do, any schedule I had to keep. I was not happy.

Churches started calling me to an interim pastor position. The third church that called was the Trinity Baptist Church in Sun City Center, Florida, a retirement community. It was 39 miles away and was a senior adult church. I had never pastored a senior adult church, but I found I liked some of their practices. They had no meetings at night. Deacon meetings and all committees met in the afternoon. I loved that and accepted the interim pastor position. After a month, they called me to be their pastor. I served there for ten years, and God blessed. I was used to a lot of young people and babies. We didn't have any young people or babies. I learned quickly what it took to build that church. The church doubled in size, we enlarged the parking area, built a new building, and erected a very nice sign on the highway.

As you might guess, we had a lot of friends. Our minister of music was a very godly man and we worked well together reaching seniors. We also had out-of-state trips and the seniors loved that as well. Every five years you might think of taking a group to Israel. We always tried to get the seniors to travel with and eat with people in our church that they did not know well. The new friendships that were established really helped our group to grow.

We had a senior adult softball team that played in a league the city established. We had ladies from the church come and be cheerleaders. If you have a bowling alley in your town, start a team. Establish a bridge group that would play in a city building or a restaurant.

Establish home Bible studies. Be careful who your teachers are. Use only people that have proven themselves over the years in your church. Encourage senior men to be deacons. Many of our seniors have a world of experience and a close walk with the Lord. Don't count them out in places of leadership in your church.

Encourage your senior men who are willing to be a deacon to start a coffee or breakfast group with other senior men at a local restaurant. These groups can be established and last for a lifetime. It is also a great place to invite visitors to your church. The visitors will sit with different folks each week or month and establish new friendships. Many will be led to Christ through these groups.

Senior adults love to be noticed and included in meetings with their pastor. If your church finances are capable to do this, establish a fund where the pastor and his wife can take out visiting couples to lunch on Sunday. About half the couples we took out and I paid for their lunch joined our church. Almost all of them said they were used to buying their pastor and his wife lunch rather than the other way around.

Seniors love to be asked for their opinion about something. I was asking seniors questions all the time. We asked senior couples over to our home a lot. That made them feel wanted and loved.

When I visited senior adult prospects, I learned to stay a while. When I visited them in the hospital, I stayed a while. I called all of them two days after they went home from the hospital.

I tried to go to all the small group parties. It was a great place to visit and to converse in a very casual setting. I would make my way around the room and have a conversation with every person there.

My door at the church was always open to those who wanted to talk. I never made people set up an appointment three or four days later. If someone tried to monopolize my time, I would tell my visitor that I needed to go to the hospital. I truly always did need to visit the hospital and see someone.

I would preach a sermon about heaven every year. A lot of seniors think about their afterlife often. You want to assure them that God has a wonderful place prepared for them and that all their pains physically and relationally will be left behind on earth. Jeremiah 29:11 is such a great text and a great promise that every believer can count on.

I have always had retired ministers in my churches. I tried to visit with them and tell them how much they meant to the kingdom of God. I would get them to tell me stories of their days in various churches. I would call on them to pray at various services and help with the Lord's Supper if they wanted to do it.

These retired ministers should be honored and loved in our churches. I like to call on our senior adults for advice on various issues. Many times these seniors will have great ideas that can help your church. I also ask them to visit with our shut-in members. If you can designate one senior to every shut-in member, it will be a blessing for each person that is involved in that ministry.

At least once a year in a Sunday morning service I asked every church member to remember to put their church in their will. Seniors will do this if you ask them to do it.

You can have a senior adult choir in your church. This will be a place for your seniors to serve in ministry. They will love it and will love you for promoting it. Get a senior adult quartet going. Get them to have matching clothes. They will love it.

Another activity for senior adults is what I call "A Night of Fine Dining", as I outlined in the chapter on Single Adult Ministries. Pick out six nice restaurants and get your seniors to plan ahead for a year-and-a-half. Each quarter, get the participants to meet at the church and carpool to the restaurant. Encourage everyone to dress up a little. Many seniors have some very nice clothes but have no occasion to wear them. Widows often miss going out to nice restaurants because they don't want to go alone. This gives them a chance to go with a group, meet new friends, and dress up. Do this four times a year and promote it in your newsletter and your Sunday morning service. Spending one whole evening with people you don't know establishes new friends. Try not to have people drive to the restaurant alone.

Many seniors do not know anything about computers. Have a class at the church and get some of your computer savvy members to teach the class. Once again, the seniors will meet with people they do not know, and friendships will be established. This is a great ministry, and you can invite people who are not members of your church. The more you promote this class, the more people you don't know will participate. This can be a great evangelistic opportunity. Develop classes teaching English. Develop classes that help people with their tax forms. Many times, the leaders can lead them to Jesus through the ministry of these classes.

In my first full-time church, there were many very interesting people. I had three retired pastors and two retired ministers of music. There was also a retired scholar who had written many books and held high offices in the Baptist Convention. They all tried to help me, and I really appreciated all that they said.

Two ladies in that church had worked in the mission's area of the Baptist Convention. They both worked over 40 years in their positions. They both were retired and were in their late 70's.

I tried to visit every member in my first year at that church. As I got down to the last 25 people, I went to see one of those elderly denominational workers. She was very nice and we told each other of our backgrounds. The conversation went on for over an hour, and then the lady asked me an odd question. She said, "How are your finances?" I didn't know how to answer that question. She then said, "Are you putting money in the retirement program of our denomination?" I said "Yes, but not very much."

She said, "You ought to be putting in the maximum amount." I didn't know what to say next. She told me her life story and that she also had put in very little on a monthly basis. She said, "Now I am in poverty. They gave me a plaque when I retired. You can't buy food or clothes with a plaque. I'm on welfare and my life is sad. You need to start this week getting your financial house in order." We talked for another twenty minutes and then I left.

For the next three or four days, I thought about my financial situation and wondered if I was going to be in poverty and live on welfare. My entire life savings to this point was a total of $500.

About two weeks later, I went to see the other older lady that had worked for our denomination for over 40 years. She was very nice, and we had a wonderful conversation. She then said, "Are you saving up some money for your retirement?" I said, "Well, I have started putting some money into our denomination retirement plan." She said, "You have to put in more than $10 a month if you want to have a happy retirement. Put in the maximum amount and you will be much happier when you retire. The program is a good one, and if you participate wisely, the program will be a blessing to you."

I thought about what they had said for three or four days, and then I made a major decision in my life. I found out what the maximum amount was that I could contribute and I sent it monthly for over 45 years. My wife and I now have a great retirement income. Those two elderly ladies really, really helped their young pastor. I will be forever indebted to these senior adult ladies who literally changed my life!

Chapter 15
About My Schedule

I retired after pastoring the same church for 21 years. The next month I just about went crazy. I was used to getting up at 7 a.m., visiting all the sick people on Monday, visiting the visitors late Monday night, if it was not too late, and visiting on Tuesday until all of our visitors were visited. On Wednesday, I met with staff, decided on scripture for my Sunday morning service, and studied for my Wednesday night Bible study. Then on Thursday I called all the people in the hospital and visited those in the hospital that I had not already seen. Friday was my day off and I studied at home all day for my Sunday morning service, took my wife out to eat Friday night, and usually invited a prospect family to join us.

On Saturday, I would study for my Sunday morning sermon and take breaks by watching sports on T.V., and continue studying until about 11 p.m. I got up on Sunday at 6 a.m. and studied my Sunday morning sermon again until 8:30 a.m. Then I would meet folks at church coming in at the main door. After preaching both morning services, I usually took out prospects for lunch, and about 70% of those people joined the church. My wife was a tremendous asset in this process. Everyone loved her. Up until the last few years, I had also taught a Sunday School class in between sermons. I loved the intimacy of our class but needed to stop as I grew older to preserve my voice for preaching.

On Sunday afternoon I studied for my Sunday night sermon. I arrived 30 minutes before the evening service and greeted everyone as they came in. We were blessed to have an amazing minister of music who always had great music not only Sunday morning but also on Sunday night that often included different ensembles and children's choirs that helped build up the crowd. After the service, many of us went out to a local restaurant to eat together. When other churches had stopped their Sunday night services due to low attendance, our attendance remained strong and consistent due to the Holy Spirit and the consistent effort that we put into the worship experience.

After having the same schedule for over 40 years, it was <u>very</u> hard to retire. Three weeks later I was pastoring another church. Ten years later I retired again, and it was very hard to adjust. I like to work.

Many times, in ministry we take our eye off the ball and let the distractions of life take over our time schedule. In Hebrews 12:1 we read these words, "Let us throw off everything that hinders and the sin that so easily entangles, and let us run with perseverance the race marked out for us."

Those last words are so important, "the race marked out for us." God has uniquely planned many things in your life. No one can run your race for you. Only you can run that race. The writer of Hebrews tells us that if we are going to successfully run the race, we will have to remove all distractions.

When I was in seminary, there was a guy in our class named Jim Patterson. He had gone to college on a golf scholarship. When he would go play golf with some of our fellow seminarians, they all hated to play with him. He concentrated on every shot. He never talked. He was all business on the golf course. The rest of the guys liked to talk and cut up. Not Jim, he was concentrating. He removed all distractions from his mind. Not only was Jim no fun to play with, he <u>always</u> won. Did you watch Tiger Woods and Phil Mickelson play in all those championships? It was the same thing—no talking, all concentration, and removing all distractions.

Hebrews 12:1 says that sin entangles us or distracts us. The only one that can do something about the sin that distracts you in your life is you. We must focus on the important things. Do them first. Visit the dying first. Return calls quickly. Keep your schedule. Don't forget your family. Concentrate.

Chapter 16
Personal Integrity

If you are starting out in ministry, your finances are important. They will determine what your children can do, and if you can take care of health bills when you are older. Early in my ministry when people wanted to give me some money for a wedding or a funeral or something else, I always said, "No thanks, that is part of my job." That was a mistake. If people want to give you some money, take it. That is a blessing for them.

What you should <u>not</u> do is to ask people in your church for money and gifts for yourself and your family. Some pastors even write back to former churches and ask friends there to help them or their children financially. Both of these practices are unethical and cause problems in the church. If someone is kind enough to offer a lake or beach house for your use, be gracious and accept. However, leave it nicer than you found it or offer to pay for the cleaning after use. Be sure not to take advantage--let them offer it again without you asking. Send a nice thank you note telling how much your family enjoyed their generosity.

Don't think that you can analyze in your mind every situation that is going to come up. While pastoring in Florida, my church had two morning services. We were on the radio for 50 miles in every direction.

One Sunday morning I was surprised to see a pastor from a church about five miles away. He came to the early service each week. I preached the same sermon in both services. As I was preaching, he was obviously writing something down. He did that during my whole sermon. When our service was over, as always, I went to the front door of the church to say good-bye to everyone and visit with some. That pastor never came to the door where I was standing.

There was a family in the other pastor's church that were all very religious people. Their grandmother, who was a member but could not attend because she was crippled, stayed home and listened to the various ministers that preached on the radio. The rest of the family went to the 11 o'clock service.

On a particular Sunday, when all the family came home from their church, the grandmother couldn't wait to tell them a funny story that she had heard on the radio. She began to tell them the story, and all of a sudden, they interrupted her and finished the same story. Their pastor told the story as if it had all happened to him.

The grandmother then began to tell other things about the sermon. It was very obvious that their pastor had preached the same sermon that I had preached at our 10 o'clock service. Someone in the family squealed about what their pastor had done, particularly saying that he took my personal illustrations, and said that these were events that had happened to him. As you might imagine, this caused the pastor at that church a lot of trouble.

I was amazed that the pastor could write down as much as he could and preach the same sermon an hour later. It always took me about 12 hours to get prepared. I'm sure he suffered for this mistake. God teaches us in many different ways.

Be careful to treat everyone with graciousness and kindness. You should honor everyone from the server at a local restaurant to the CEO of a large company. No matter what happens, give a little more than the standard tip. If you think you received poor service, don't go back, but still leave a good tip. The worst thing you can do is leave a track about salvation and then shortchange the server. Encourage your members to be generous as well.

One of the most important areas of integrity is faithfulness to your wife and family. Even as a single pastor, you must guard your integrity and not even give the appearance of impropriety. I made it a rule to not counsel a woman alone without my secretary present in the office with us or I would leave the door cracked open with the secretary just outside. If counseling after hours could not be avoided, I invited my wife to join us.

Sometimes even the best plans cannot prepare you for all the snares laid by the devil and you have to think fast on your feet. As a single pastor who didn't cook, I loved and cultivated my friendships with families and enjoyed going into their homes for meals. It was one of the highlights of ministry to get to fellowship over some good home cooking. One couple I will call "Joe and Sue" had hosted me several times for meals. Sue came up to me at church and said that she had made my favorite pie, pecan, and that they would like me to come over for a piece. I showed up at the appointed time and walked in the door. I saw only Sue and said, "Where's Joe?" She told me he was out of town for work. I asked, "Where are the kids?" She said that they were spending the night at their friends. I then said, "Where's the pie?" I inhaled the pie in about 30 seconds and told her that I had to leave immediately for an appointment. A week later, Sue came up to me at church and said that she felt badly that I had to leave so fast the last time and that she had baked another pie and invited me to come back to their home. I thanked her and said that I would check my calendar and let her know. I waited until she was standing next to her husband Joe at church and said loudly, "Sue, I can't come over for pie on Tuesday April 29th at 4:30 pm. I have a lot on my calendar." She never asked me again.

Chapter 17
The Power Of Prayer

The purpose of prayer is emphatically not to bend God's will to ours, but rather to align our will to His.

Have you ever prayed for the wrong thing? I watched a movie as a boy and the star of the movie had a big scar across his chest, and another big scar across his face. I thought that was very manly. He was a strong man and I wanted to be like him.

I prayed for three weeks every night to be strong and have scars like the man in the movie. I wanted my masculinity to be obvious and impressive. After praying for three weeks every night, I gave up. What have you prayed for that was so important and so wrong? As we mature in our faith, our prayers mature as well.

I read about a little boy who was asked to pray before the Sunday lunch. All the family was in place around the table and all the heads were bowed. The boy looked over the meal set on the table, and instead of bowing his head to pray, he picked up his fork and started eating. His parents spoke up and asked him why he didn't pray before he started to eat. The boy answered, "I already prayed for this food, these are leftovers."

I had a good friend in Dallas, Texas, many years ago named Gary Carter. Gary had cerebral palsy and had tremendous difficulty doing anything. His brain was sharp, but his body was all messed up. Gary's father was a medical doctor, and his mother was a well-educated, beautiful, healthy woman. <u>The Carters never helped Gary do anything</u>. He had to button his own shirt, even though it took him six minutes. The thing that really bothered all of us that regularly dropped by to visit with Gary was that the Carters didn't even help Gary when he fell down, which was often. He had to get up by himself. The Carters never helped him.

The Carters' love was demonstrated by not doing for him what he could do for himself. Doctors and therapists had counseled the Carters to respond in that way. If they always helped him, he would become, over time, completely helpless.

As the years passed, Gary learned to drive a car, cook, and even get a job. He was a remarkable, wonderful young man. Though this sounds strange, God blessed Gary in many ways. Many of us pray for good health and then we abuse our bodies. Stop asking God to do something for you that you can do for yourself.

Many years ago, I lived in an apartment very close to the Dobbins Air Reserve Base in Marietta, Georgia. At about 10 p.m. on a Saturday night, I was studying my sermon for the next day. Suddenly, I heard a very strange noise. It sounded like a sick helicopter. I listened, and the noise got closer and closer and closer. I suddenly realized that helicopter was coming right for my apartment. When some extraordinary event is happening, your mind has the capacity to think very quickly. I believe I made about four distinct prayers in about four seconds. They were as follows:

> 1. Lord, please don't let that helicopter hit my home. (I realized later that was so self-centered.)
> 2. I thought of all the kids that lived close by and prayed, "Lord, please don't let it him them."
> 3. Lord, it's okay if it hits my home, but please don't let it hit me (I was back to the self-centered stuff).
> 4. Lord, thank you (when the sound passed over).

About three more seconds passed and I heard the helicopter crash. About 200 yards from my home, the helicopter hit two trees. The air force men were onboard, but they walked away unharmed.

When things get crucial, we can really pray, can't we? Let me say, today things are crucial. All sorts of people are trying to blow us up, cheat us, break up our marriages, and destroy our families. During the Covid difficulty, many politicians wanted to keep the Christians away from church but allowed the strip clubs to remain open. Americans face real crises today: health issues, the failure of government and social systems, socialism gaining ground, and enemies who hate us.

When crisis comes, please, Lord, guide us.

Chapter 18

The Pastor's Prayers Are Important

If you are going to a new church to be their pastor, your prayer life is of great importance. You might ask yourself as you drive onto the church property for the first time, "Who should I pray for?" or "What should I pray for?" or "With whom should I pray?" Let me give you some suggestions.

- You should pray for your whole church every day.
- Pray with and for your wife and children every day.
- You should find out who is in the hospital from your new church your first day there. You should go to the hospital and pray with them your second day there. I know you have to unpack all of your stuff and get the electricity turned on and another hundred other things that are important, but the folks that are in the hospital will never forget that their new pastor came to see them the second day of being at the church. The folks in the hospital will tell their friends what you did.
- Get your church secretary to call all the homebound people and find out when you can come to their homes to pray for them and with them. <u>Don't wait to be asked</u>. They will never forget how quickly your ministry touched their lives. They will tell their friends what you did. Get your church secretary to call all the new church visitors and set up a time for you to come to their homes and pray with them and for them.

Take your wife or one of the church deacons or leaders with you. Over your first few weeks, begin to take some of your Bible study leaders with you to see your church visitors. Pray with the Bible study leaders or deacons or church leaders in your car before you go into the visitor's homes.

• Pray with your church staff every week. Before you pray, ask the staff if they have prayer concerns, they want to share. Over the years, I have worked with a lot of people who were ministers of music, educational ministers, youth ministers, children's ministers, or some other specific area of ministry. I have been close friends with at least fifty pastors. If you stay in ministry for many years, you will have various staff members disappoint you. You will have various deacons and Bible study leaders disappoint you. Pray with them before they are corrected and after they are corrected. A preacher many years ago told me when I had to remove a leader my attitude should be to hate the sin and love the sinner. I have tried to follow that advice.

• Many of your church members believe James 5:16(The Living Translation). It says, "The earnest prayer of a righteous man has great power and wonderful results." Many of your church members think of you as their righteous man. They want to hear you pray for them, their church, and their country. Your prayers are <u>so</u> important.

- We need to pray for God to lead us into doing *great* things. Don't ever be satisfied with how things are. Set up three goals in your heart and head. As you pray about those three things that God has placed in your mind, begin taking steps toward seeing those three things happen. If your church family has no vision or goals for the future, the church will get smaller and smaller. Pray that God will touch your church leaders' hearts and guide them to lead out in godly goals. They will all want to know what you think about the future. Spell it out for them and send a letter to every church member explaining what is going on and what part they can take to make the goals happen. Ask them to pray every day for God's direction and power as the church moves forward.
- Other pastors are important, and you should pray for them. Pastors that are in your community or county are people that you should meet. Pastors in your denomination in your area can be of great help to you and you should want to meet them as soon as possible. Each pastor has strengths and weaknesses just as you do. These other pastors can answer many of your questions about what works and what doesn't work in that area. Perhaps you can learn from them about resources that would help your ministry.

When you go to a church as a pastor, you will meet pastors of small churches in the area that are struggling in ministry. Maybe you can help them by becoming a friend. Let them know that you are praying for them and their family. Perhaps there will be pastors of large churches in the area that will take time to help you. Listen to them and learn from them.

Perhaps after a year of ministry you realize that things are not going well at your church. If you have developed friendships with pastors of large churches, they might help you to go to another church as pastor or go to a large church as a staff member. Maybe you could become a youth minister or a missions' minister. It takes all of us a period of time to be in the right church doing the right thing. God will open doors for us. We need to pray daily for doors to open.

When I was on the staff of a large church in Dallas, I served as a singles minister. The pastor hired a young man to be the youth minister about five months after I started serving that church. The youth minister that was hired had never been a youth minister before. He did not know what he was doing and things in his area began to fall apart. Every week at staff meeting the pastor of that church put a piece of paper in front of each chair where the different ministers sat. On that piece of paper two numbers were listed: the number of people present in your area (like youth ministry, or singles ministry, or choir, or nursery) one year ago and the number of people present in your area of ministry the day before (our staff meetings were on Monday mornings at nine o'clock). The pastor would ask the person to his left to tell why his number was either up or down from the year before. The youth minister's numbers seemed to go down week after week. The youth minister would stop by the restroom each week before our staff meeting and throw up and cry. I realized what was happening one week when I stopped by the restroom on my way to the staff meeting. Later that day, I went to the youth minister's office and prayed with him and tried to help in some way. About three months later, the pastor fired the youth minister. (Incidentally, the pastor should never fire anyone. Refer the issues to the personnel committee or the chairman of the deacons and let them fire someone.)

The pastor of that church had not prayed with that youth minister. I learned a lot from that pastor. I mostly learned what not to do, one of which was not to pit staff members against each other.

The pastor's prayers are so important.

Chapter 19
Dealing With Problems In Your Church

If you are having staff meetings, or church business meetings, or deacons' meetings, or division meetings (like all the preschool leadership, or all of the senior adult leadership, or all of the high school leadership) and people are yelling, the yellers need to be told that they are losing the argument, even if they have the facts and history on their side.

The new pastor should <u>never</u> yell about anything unless it is a sporting event. If you yell, that will always be remembered by everyone who was present. Count to ten or something else, but don't yell at meetings. Be friendly with everyone in the room, even if they hold an opinion opposite of yours. Remember, there will be another day, another argument, and another opportunity for you to show your maturity and wisdom.

When you first go to a church, make friends with the leaders. Show your love for all the age groups. Support the existing staff. Don't try to change 18 things your first year in your new church. Don't oppose the old people time and time again. I know many new pastors who just want pictures of younger people in their advertisements. The older people paid for the buildings, the land, and a hundred other things that have helped the church to stay alive. Thank them, honor them, listen to them, and try to keep them happy.

Many times, information overcomes objection. Try to explain every new step you want to take in the church. Get some older people who agree with what you are trying to accomplish at the church to explain it in their Bible study class and perhaps at one of their class parties. Get the word out numerous times what you want to see done before you present it to the church. Any major changes at the church will be a problem for many of the people. I have always said when I was proposing something new, "If it doesn't work, we will change it back. It has worked at a lot of other churches."

If many people are <u>very</u> hostile to your idea, put it off six months. By then, you will have led some more people to Jesus and made friends with some people you didn't really know when you first presented your idea of change. Be friendly to your critics. Visit them and members of their families when they are sick or in the hospital. Your love will be received well.

Sometimes God will surprise you and bless your idea about change. After you have three or four of these situations work out well under your leadership, just keep a steady hand on the wheel and the people will pray for you and follow you.

It is a major problem if you lock into a certain attitude about two or three people in your church who always seem to be against whatever you are trying to get the church to do. If you think they will never be different, you are building a block in your own mind that will not be helpful for the future. All of the important things (ideals, plans, hopes) can be altered in life. In <u>Hope For the Separated</u> by Dr. Gary Chapman, he says, "We are not a deterministic people, we believe in hope. God can help us change patterns in our lives that have been in us for generations." The people in your church can change their minds and come to the place where they agree with you about changes in your church and even can come to love and appreciate you. You have to stay a while for this to happen.

Dr. Chapman says that "All of us have pent up emotions and opinions that have festered for a long time. The force of those feelings works against reconciliation." If we are going to deal with problems in the church, we have to be openminded, willing to listen to others, and realize that everyone is not going to agree with us.

I pastored a church in Fayetteville, Georgia many years ago. The church desperately needed more parking. The church owned property right next to the church. On that land there were over 15 <u>very</u> large and <u>very</u> old trees. They were beautiful and meant a lot to many people. There was no other clear property adjacent to our church. I felt like we had to make that large lot a place for parking. Our church was growing, and it seemed to me that it was obvious what we needed to do.

I talked to a number of leaders in the church, and they all agreed with me that we really needed that property for parking. One of the men volunteered to bring his bulldozer up to the church and knock down all the trees. I asked him if he would get in trouble for doing that. He replied that he was friends with all of the city council members. I said, "God bless you, brother."

One day that week he got to the church very early on a very large bulldozer. In about four or five hours he knocked down all the trees. As that day passed, many people came to look at what had been done. Numerous people were really angry. They all blamed me. Later in the day, a lady came into my office and said a number of inappropriate words. She told me those trees had been there long before I was born. She went on and on, and I said nothing. After about an hour, I said my first words. I asked her, "Are those trees more important than souls?" She looked at me for about five minutes and then said, "I would have to think that over."

After about three weeks, we paved that lot. Our Bible study and worship services both grew immediately. That lady never spoke to me again. The church continued to grow. We filled the parking lot.

Every church has problems. I decided to always talk with our church staff first and our deacons second. We would pray about it and deal with the problem.

Every church has some problem people in it. The new pastor has to deal with and live with those people. One of the churches I pastored had a man in it that thought he was in charge of the town, all of the activities in the town, and he thought he was in charge of our church.

After I had been there for two weeks, he called me and told me he wanted to buy my lunch. I accepted his offer immediately. I met him at a nice restaurant, and we had a nice conversation. He told me of the major accomplishments in his life. I was impressed. He asked me about the major accomplishments in my life. I responded by trying to sound humble, but I did mention that I had earned a doctorate and every church that I had pastored, through the grace of God, had doubled in size.

He didn't seem impressed at all by what I had said, and he didn't make any comments about what I had said. He drove a few miles in silence and then looked at me and said, "You do the weddings and the funerals, and I will run the church." At first, I thought he was kidding. I didn't say anything. He wasn't kidding. He was chairman of the deacons, and he was running the church. I found that out in my first month at the church.

We started having a lot of visitors at the church. I guess they wanted to hear the new preacher. I visited every visitor I could. People started joining the church. Our sanctuary was small and there was very little parking space. Many of the pastors before me at that church had wanted to build a new sanctuary and add many more parking places. The man that was running the church did not want that to happen.

People continued to join the church and it was obvious that we needed a new sanctuary and many more parking places. I started mentioning in sermons and at deacons' and committees' meetings the need for expansion needed to start. Finally, a committee was formed to purchase property and build a new sanctuary. The same gentleman continued to oppose everything I wanted to do. People continued to join the church. Eventually, the property was purchased, and the huge sanctuary was built.

After I had been at the church for four years, one Sunday morning in the vestibule the same man walked up to me and said, "You have been here for four years. That is long enough. It is time for you to go." I said, "Have a great day, brother." I stayed 21 years. I never argued with him.

I found out years later he had told other pastors that had come to that church to do the weddings and funerals and he would run the church. None of them stayed very long.

Another interesting thing happened at that church when I first came on view of a call. A middle-aged couple told everyone to vote against me because I was single. Many of those that heard what the couple had said, told me. I went to their home (the middle-aged couple) to visit and find out why they were so opposed to be single person being their pastor. They said the Bible said the pastor should be married. I asked them where in the Bible does it say a pastor should be married. They said everyone knows that a pastor should be married. I responded that Paul and Jesus were single, so it must be all right. They left the church and never came back.

Five years later, a single lady that ran a home for wayward teenage girls visited our church with 25 teenage girls. I met her, a beautiful and godly lady, and I thought, "I wish she was older." She was 25 and I was 45. As time passed, we dated, fell in love, and married. There were over 1500 at our wedding. The middle-aged couple was not there.

There is one other weird problem person I want to mention. In my first full-time church there was a very strange, but harmless, lady. She stayed awake all night and slept all day. Her husband slept all night and stayed awake all day. She asked me one day if it was all right for her to call me at night. I said, "Of course, call me anytime you want to." That was a huge mistake. Let me say that again, that was a huge mistake!

The first time she called me at 1 a.m. I talked with her for about one hour. She then started calling about twice a week and wanted the conversation to go on and on. I developed a plan. When she would call, I would talk with her for about ten minutes. I would then ask her to hold on for a few minutes. Every time she called, I asked her to hold on five minutes longer. I would set my alarm and go back to sleep. I told her I was very busy at night and continued to add five minutes to the amount of time she would have to hold the phone. When it got to the place where she was holding the phone for over an hour, she stopped calling.

Another problem person issue is when some person or persons decide they have a new understanding of the Bible and they want everyone else to buy into their new theological perspective. To illustrate this problem, there were about five people in one of my churches where I served a pastor, who decided that we should only pay attention to what Paul had written. They believed that everything else in the Bible should be set aside. I spent a lot of time writing a sermon that refuted that point of view. I preached that sermon on a Sunday morning and handed a copy of that sermon to those with that perspective.

Whenever some individual or group of people decide they have a new perspective on some Biblical issue or translation of some chapter in the Bible, be sure your examination of that perspective is thorough. For over 2,000 years scholars have been studying every verse and every chapter of God's Word. Don't quickly accept some new idea or theological position.

Chapter 20
Don't Run Off All The People In The Church That You Don't Like

Years ago, a very close, godly friend of mine joined a "Bible Church." The church was small, and my friend became an elder there. Two or three of the members decided that the pastor was not spiritual enough to be their pastor. My friend began the process of excommunicating those that wanted to fire the pastor.

He followed the biblical plan in Matthew 18:15-17.

Step 1. Go to the person privately, tell him how he has sinned against you or the church. Tell him he can be reconciled if he is willing. If the offending person repents, no more action is required.

Step 2. If the person won't listen, go back with two or three witnesses to have the conversation again, establishing the facts and the evidence.

Step 3. If he still refuses to listen and repent from his sinfulness, bring him before the full church body and make the case against him.

Step 4. If there is still no repentance, the church is to excommunicate the sinner.

After the biblical steps were taken, those that wanted to fire the pastor were excommunicated.

As time passed, another small group didn't like how some things were going in the church. That small group decided to call all the members of the church and complain how things were going at their church. This, of course, caused great turmoil in the church. The pastor and the elders decided to excommunicate that small group. After taking the biblical steps, that small group was excommunicated. The church began to lose members. A few months passed and a certain lady in the church decided she would speak out at all meetings and let the church know what she thought about everything. She thought she had the answer for all questions in the church. A number of people in the church told her to tone it down, but she would not do that. The leaders of the church decided to excommunicate her. That action was taken, and many more people left the church. A few months later, the church closed.

Another excommunication story happened in Plant City, Florida, when I was pastor at First Baptist Church. One of the smaller churches on the edge of town had a pastor that felt like he should dictate what everyone should do. He particularly felt like no women should have any authority in the church. Mrs. Dossey was a very godly woman and was one of the most active ladies in the church. She knew and loved everyone in the church. As time passed, she and the pastor began to express different opinions about different issues. The pastor told Mrs. Dossey to quit speaking out against what he thought. She suggested that the church vote on the matters that were being discussed. The pastor did not want to do that, and he called the deacons to come and meet with him. The pastor said he had talked with Mrs. Dossey and she was not going to agree with everything he said. He said that she was disruptive, and she planned to continue to speak out against him. The pastor said they should excommunicate her.

As the time for a church vote drew closer, the pastor decided to excommunicate Mr. Dossey as well. When the vote happened, both Mr. and Mrs. Dossey were excommunicated. About five families from that church visited the church I was pastoring the next Sunday. I visited each family in their homes. During the next month, more families from that church visited us. On about the seventh Sunday, fifteen families came down the aisle and joined our church.

On Monday, Mr. Dossey came in to see me at the church and wanted to explain to me about his giving to the church. He said he had made a substantial pledge to the church that had just excommunicated him and his wife. He said he tithed all his life, but he wanted to pay off the pledge that he had made to his former church. He said he would be tithing soon to our church. I was impressed. This man followed through with the commitment he had made to the Lord.

I have seen many times how a new pastor comes to a church, and he wants to change many things right away. He might want the church to move from traditional music to contemporary music in three months. When people in the church come by to complain about the radical change in the music ministry, and the pastor or minister of music has an attitude of "this is the way it's going to be, and if you don't like it, there are other churches in the area," get ready for people to leave your church. Many of the people that leave might be the people that are great bible study leaders, great soloists, or great givers, or people that have led a lot of people to Jesus.

You need to know who you are running off before you run them off. Some people are great prayer warriors. You really don't want to run them off, or the people that they have mentored to be great prayer warriors. Some people in your new church have designated all their money and all of their homes, cars, etc., to the church. You do not want to run those people off.

I have tried to be friendly to those who have been rude to me or to my wife. I try not to run anyone off. I have seen people change over the years. I remember people that had said terrible things about me or about my wife. As the years passed, they observed that each year hundreds of people were making a profession of faith and joining the church. They also saw new buildings built and more parking areas developed. They watched as I performed their children's weddings or their parents' funerals. They saw me at the hospital when I stood at their bedside and prayed for health to improve.

Many of those people over the years quit being an antagonist and became a supporter. If you just stay at a church for two or three years, you will miss the blessing of seeing people mature spiritually over the years. You will also miss feeling like you are part of so many families.

Chapter 21
Keep The Main Thing The Main Thing

I once heard a friend of mine preach a sermon on Mount Gerizim. The mountain is in Samaria. It is 2,849 feet high. Moses commanded that when the Israelites came into the Promised Land, the blessing for keeping the law should be spoken from Mount Gerizim. From the top of Mount Gerizim, Jotham shouted his parable of the trees to the men of Shechem in the valley below, remind them of all that his father, Gideon, had done for them.

My friend preached for 45 minutes. Forty of those minutes were about Mount Gerizim. He told us many facts that most of us had never heard. I thought it was a terrible sermon. No one made a profession of faith. No one joined the church. No one cared too much about Mount Gerizim. He didn't keep the main thing the main thing.

Years ago, a pastor invited me to come to his church in Dallas and preach a weekend revival. I preached on Friday night and Saturday night and Sunday morning. He asked me to stay over Sunday night so that I could hear him preach that evening. He was preaching a six-month series on the Ark of the Covenant. What he did had no relation to the topic of the revival. I just think he wanted me to see his preparation and creativity and depth of knowledge about the Ark of the Covenant.

The Sunday morning service went well. Decisions for Christ were made. On Sunday afternoon, the pastor had trained about ten men to come to the sanctuary and remove all the furniture around the Lord's Supper table along with removing the chairs and sound equipment. After everything was out of the way, the men added portable walls and curtains and podiums and candles and many other things. It looked like the Ark of the Covenant. All the things that were brought in were facing Jerusalem (in the United States, the east). All the prayers in the service were directed toward the east.

The pastor had the congregation rise whenever the holy portion of the wall they had constructed was opened to remove the sacred scrolls of the Law. They tried to set up the Ark in a way that it could be visible from every part of the sanctuary. It was considered as symbolic of the Holy of Holies in the Jerusalem Temple. I thought that what they did was interesting, but certainly not to be done every Sunday night for six months. They were not keeping the main thing the main thing.

Philippians 3:7-12 is a good rule of thumb for us, "*7* But all these things that I once thought very worthwhile—now I've thrown them all away so that I can put my trust and hope in Christ alone. *8* Yes, everything else is worthless when compared with the priceless gain of knowing Christ Jesus my Lord. I have put aside all else, counting it worth less than nothing, in order that I can have Christ *9* and become one with Him, no longer counting on being saved by being good enough or by obeying God's laws, but by trusting Christ to save me; for God's way of making us right with Himself depends on faith—counting on Christ alone. *10* Now I have given up everything else—I have found it to be the only way to really know Christ and to experience the mighty power that brought Him back to life again, and to find out what it means to suffer and to die with Him. *11* So whatever it takes, I will be one who lives in the fresh newness of life of those who are alive from the dead. *12* I don't mean to say I am perfect. I haven't learned all I should even yet, but I keep working toward that day when I will finally be all that Christ saved me for and wants me to be."

Many of our pastors are creative and they want to do something new. It is fine to do something new, but we want to remember that everything we do should draw us closer to Jesus. The words and actions of Jesus and His disciples are the main thing. Every sermon and every service should lead people to Jesus or develop them in their faith. I have written all of this to help people who are going into the ministry. Some start pastoring when they feel the call of God on their hearts. Some start in ministry when they finish college or seminary.

I want to encourage you to answer God's call on your life. You will have the wonderful opportunity to lead many to Jesus. Let me close with another story that I hope will be helpful in your life.

My sophomore year at Baylor I wanted to preach every opportunity that I could. A guy in my dorm asked me to preach at his little country church in east Texas. Even though it would take two and a half hours to drive to the little church, I was ready. Another guy that I knew grew up in east Texas right around where the church was located so I asked if he would like to go because he knew his way around. We left Sunday morning before dawn. After about two hours, the sun came out and I noticed a small patch of blue on the side of the rode. A little while later I heard my friend say "One". We continued driving and there was a larger patch about ten yards wide of blue out in a field. I asked my friend what it was. He told me that they were bluebonnets and that they blossomed all over east Texas this time of year. Then I heard, "Two, three... four... five... six." We drove a few more miles and I saw more bluebonnet patches sporadically across fields and pastures and in people's yards. My friend having grown up in east Texas didn't seem to notice the flowers, but then I heard him say, "Seven...eight, nine." We came up over a ridge and I saw an entire valley of bluebonnets before us. Being from Tennessee, I had never seen anything like this before in my life. It took my breath away. I wanted to stop the car and have a moment of spiritual renewal. Then I heard, "Ten." I had had enough. I asked my friend, "What are you counting?" He replied, "The dead armadillos on the side of the rode".

Remember your brothers and sisters in the Lord are counting on you to lead them and keep 'the main thing the main thing'. My friend was a good guy, but he got used to the bluebonnets and they were not special to him anymore. He focused on the dead armadillos and missed the rich beauty of God's blessing.

As you move to new places in ministry there will be a lot of insignificant issues trying to get your attention. Make sure that you are focusing on bluebonnets and not dead armadillos.

God bless you in your service to our Lord. There will be some difficult days, but there will also be many victories for our Savior. Remember Jeremiah 29:11: "For I know the plans I have for you," declares the Lord, "plans to prosper you and not harm you, plans to give you hope and a future."

Chapter 22
Great Ideas To Get You Going

- "Heroes," said Ralph Waldo Emerson, "are no braver than ordinary people. They are just brave five minutes longer."
- Keep praying; God will bless you because you talk with Him.
- "You must love the Lord, your God, with all your heart, all your soul, all your mind, and all your strength." And "Love your neighbor as yourself." (Mark 12:30-31) Only Christ can help us do that.
- As long as we think we can bargain with God, we are sure to make ourselves a good deal.
- What if God in giving us the Ten Commandments had a magnificent and joyful purpose in mind? God is a God of life. He is not just a life preserver in times of distress. He is a God of joy and peace, prosperity, and plenty. God has not left us to wander in the darkness of our own superstitious imaginations.
- No one knows when Jesus is coming back. Matthew 24:36
- I Cor. 13:12 "I shall know even as also I am known (in heaven).
- You might feel like today that you are trapped. That is not how your story ends. Some dreams are waking up, hope is waking up; abundance is waking up.
- God is saying to you, you have struggled long enough; unexpected blessings are coming your way.

- The forces that are for you are greater than the forces that are against you.
- You can't think negative thoughts and live a positive life.
- If you will get your mind going in the right direction, your life will go in the right direction.
- What God has in your future is more than you can imagine.
- The turning point of our lives is when we stop seeking the God we want and start seeking the God who is.
- "I know, O Lord, that a man's life is not his own, it is not for man to direct his steps." Jeremiah 10:23
- Imitation is a desire for acceptance.
- Maintain openness of spirit while displaying certainty of Christian faith.
- Nobody but God isn't involved in heresy.
- The first people who saw history as purposive and linear were the Hebrews. The Hindus and the Buddhists say time is a circle.
- The number one problem in most churches in many areas is that there are not enough trained church leaders.
- God comes to us in His Word and then we come to Him in thanksgiving and praise.
- If a doctor today found a cure for cancer, millions of people would try to see him and be cured. All the planes would be filled with people trying to get to the doctor. The highways would be full. The phones of the doctor would have thousands or millions of people calling. A more important thing than any disease you might have is how your

soul is doing. Jesus can heal your soul. He can meet your eternal problems. He loves you and wants to heal you.

• To the spiritual man, spiritual things are revealed.

• Satan usually gets sick on Sunday when he sees you in church, but he usually gets well on Mondays.

• When strength is small, when personal resources are insufficient, when friends forget or mostly criticize, when we are crowded into a corner from which there is no human escape, only then do we realize who never forsakes us. Our wonderful Lord is there.

• I wonder how long it has been since you have enjoyed sacred moments with the Lord, just you and Him talking over your life. When you are close to God, the large problems of life can be resolved quickly.

• Many of us have been invalids before the Lord, confined to our own desires.

• Nahum 1:7 is a great passage for funerals. "The Lord is good, a stronghold in the day of trouble, and He knows them that trust in Him."

• Many of the world's great men have said that their best decisions were made on their knees.

• Worship is the vital breath of the Christian life.

• In a world full of no, we are a church full of yes – yes to love, yes to caring, yes to Jesus.

• Gossip is ear pollution.

• Fifty percent of people that go to the doctor have nothing wrong with them.

Counseling

- In counseling, use the most productive and the most simple process—listen. In counseling you need to deal with the immediate situation more than on the past. Deal with the here and now rather than the there and then.
- When counseling someone, that is not the preparation for change; that is the change.
- When you are counseling, encourage your counselee to express all of their feelings about their problems. The more negative the counselee is at the first, the more chances are for positive steps later.
- When you are watching or judging someone who is bragging about their spiritual gifts, do not evaluate just their form, but focus on their content. The key question is, "Does it bring honor to Jesus?" The best spiritual gift is when you give love.
- In history you notice when the Gospel is preached, women have been elevated.
- In the Old Testament, all the major leaders were married (some married too much). In the New Testament, almost all the major leaders were unmarried.
- All of us are interim pastors.
- Christians never see each other for the last time.
- A church sign read, "Be the kind of person your dog thinks you are."
- Our sins are many; His mercy is more.
- Don't be focused on how big your problems are; think how big God is.

- I'm not just pro-life, I am pro eternal life.
- You can kneel before God: but stand for our flag.
- God answers all your prayers; He doesn't always say "yes."
- Eternity is way too long to be wrong.
- You need a small group, and the small group needs you.
- About healing, see James 5:14.
- Remember, Goliath was a 40-point favorite over David.
- If I agree with you, we would both be wrong.
- In ministry, focus on objectives, not obstacles.
- On the cross Jesus said, "It is finished." (John 19:30 New King James translation) He did not say, "I am finished."
- Obedience is choosing God's choice.
- Don't judge people by their relatives.
- I am having an out-of-money experience.
- Obstacles are those frightful things you see when you take your eyes off the goal.
- You lose with potential; you win with performance.
- Losers quit when they are tired; winners quit when they have won.
- He had a preference, but he didn't let his preference overrule his purpose.
- Some people say it doesn't matter what you believe so long as you are sincere. Does that philosophy work with arithmetic? Does it work with the IRS? Would it work with a heart surgeon? Accuracy in your belief system <u>does</u> matter.
- Be a solution finder, not a problem identifier.
- Feed your faith and your doubts will starve to death.

- Don't blame someone else. Don't deny the truth. Take it like a man.
- A penny saved is not much.
- The most important thing we can do if we love people is to tell them the truth.
- Many people want to serve God, but only as advisors.
- Kindness is a language the deaf can hear, the blind can see, and the mute can speak.
- The lady said, "My husband and I divorced over religious reasons. He thought he was God, and I didn't."
- Peter Drucker once said that an organization begins to die the day it begins to be run for the insiders and not for the outsiders. That is a message for the church.
- Put your money where your belief system is.
- A self-made man always makes his head a little too big.
- Coincidence is when God chooses to remain anonymous.
- When you subsidize poverty and failure, you get more of both.
- Giving in the Bible was often public and accompanied by a personal testimony concerning the motivation for giving.
- There are 365 "fear nots" in the Bible; one for every day.
- Pride is the only disease known to man that makes everyone sick except the one that has it.
- God wants spiritual fruit, not religious nuts.
- Pastoral authority is mentioned in Hebrews 13:17.
- If you think the church is too big, sit on the 4th row and never look back.
- When we die, we move from faith to sight.

- You can sing a hundred verses of "Just As I Am" and leave just as you are.
- The liberals think it's fine to abort babies, but balk at killing terrorists.
- Don't play "Taps" over my body, play "Reveille." I am coming to attention before the Lord.
- Your first sermon in a new church ought to be from Jeremiah 29:11.

Chapter 23
Christians Must Stand And Fight Against Socialism

Dietrich Bonhoeffer was a German Lutheran pastor, theologian, and anti-Nazi dissident. His writings on Christianity's role in the secular world have become widely influential, and his book ***The Cost of Discipleship*** is described as a modern classic. He was imprisoned and later hanged because of his resistance to Hitler's Socialist Germany.

"The ultimate test of a moral society is the kind of world that it leaves to its children."

There are many heresies and ideas that try to destroy Christians and the church. As I write this book, it has been almost 50 years since Roe vs. Wade, 20 years since the 9/11 attack, now Covid 19 is dictating how we live, and socialism is taking over our country through our government, our educational systems, and social welfare systems. I am including a chapter dealing with one of these issues since our government has taken such a dramatic turn toward accepting and even promoting socialism. I believe it is important as a pastor to stand against many different issues that are in opposition to our Lord and His Church. This is one of them.

Let me ask this question. Why should we not be socialists?

Socialists and Communists always say, as they move toward taking over a country, "Don't worry, you leave us alone and we will leave you alone." The problem with that statement is that it is a lie. Whenever the socialists are in power, they gradually push Christians down and away from freedom. In many places over the years, the socialists gradually begin to kill the Christians and destroy their churches. The goal is to rely on the government for all needs and not to rely on God.

I regularly watch a program on television called "Life, Liberty, and Levin." Mark Levin is a very bright patriotic American. He is very much against socialism. Every beginning minister and long-time minister needs to understand socialism and what harm it will bring to America.

I wrote down many things that Mark Levin said on his program, and I want to share those thoughts with you.

"In Philadelphia you can go to Independence Hall. In the Independence Hall, there are two floors, the upper chamber and the lower chamber. The reason the House of Representatives is the lower chamber is because it was on the first floor. In the upper chamber is where the Senate would meet, and then down the hall is where the Supreme Court would meet. All three groups met in this little area where America was born.

Where did this idea of America come from? It came from Aristotle and Cicero. It came from the greatest minds of their era. America was at first an idea, but then it was made into a concrete reality. There has never been anything like America made on the face of the earth except here. John Lock and Montesquieu led us to have a separation of powers in our government. These men gave direction for the founding of our country. These men were well read. They were scholars. They understood what came before and didn't work.

America is great because of its respect for the individual. Private property rights are important. We work and create wealth. You can own a home. You create your own property. Your physical and mental work is important.

The socialists are all about government and their power. Whether you work in a steel mill or a drug store, or drive a truck or cut hair, whether you are white collar or blue collar, union or non-union, middle class, lower class, or upper class, whether you live in the suburbs or inner city, liberty is the key.

Where socialists are in charge, there is no liberty. Do you want liberty or tyranny?

Think about the men that fought at Lexington and Concord. Think about the men who fought in the Revolutionary War for eight-and-a-half years. They put everything on the line. Think about the Civil War where there were over 800,000 casualties on one battlefield after another.

Remember Abraham Lincoln and his speech at Gettysburg and his second inaugural address. Think about our last century where we were attacked by the Marxists coming out of Germany. Think about World War I and World War II where we saved the world. Think about the Vietnam War and the Korean War, and all the other wars that we fought, and the thousands and thousands of people that gave their lives in all those wars. What did we fight for? Did we fight for free college or higher taxes? Did we fight for open borders? Did we fight for illegal aliens coming into America? Did we fight for Antifa so they could burn our buildings down and tear down all of our statutes?

No, we didn't. We fought for our nation and our unity, and for our values. Should we think about and follow Benjamin Franklin, Thomas Jefferson, George Washington, James Madison, and Ronald Reagan? Or should we follow the socialists to our destruction?"

Mark Levin should be heard across our land.

If we become a socialist country, we are doomed. Our children and grandchildren are being taught that socialism is the answer for everything. Every pastor and church member needs to speak out against socialism being taught in the schools. Vote for people who will take a strong stand against socialism.

About sixty years ago, Venezuela was fourth on the world's economic freedom index. Recently they are 179th and their citizens are dying from starvation. They are literally eating from other people's garbage cans. In only ten years Venezuela was destroyed by socialism.

People still think Denmark and Sweden and Norway are wonderful and joyful socialistic economies. There is one country that keeps popping up in the debates, Denmark, particularly, and, to a lesser extent, the other Nordic countries. They say that in Denmark generous benefits are given to their citizens, including affordable education for all at a very low cost, and free healthcare for all, and subsidized childcare for all.

These northern European countries enjoy a reputation for being peaceful, egalitarian, progressive, liberal, and educated in a superb way. Toward the end of the 1980's, the money ran out for all of these countries. The blue clouds turned dark and never-ending joy ended. People still think that Denmark and Sweden are socialistic economies. The prime minister of Denmark actually had to come out and say, "We are a market economy; we are not socialists."

Socialism is a very attractive thought to young people today where everything is free. In history, however, wherever socialism is, heartache soon follows. Adolph Hitler came as a man of peace and prosperity. He was a socialist. That is what Nazi means (National Socialist German Workers' Party). He produced a river of blood, a nightmare of broken futures.

Fifty million people died because of Hitler and his dreams of utopia under socialism. Joseph Stalin was a socialist. He killed thirty million Russians trying to convince the populace that his brand of socialism would really make Russia the outstanding country in the world.

Nothing has ever come out of socialism that was a blessing to the world. It is very detrimental, destructive, economically deadly, and corrupt morally and spiritually. Venezuela and Cuba and many other places are having thousands of people die. They tried socialism and it didn't work. Russia and China are helping those countries, but freedom is not the outcome.

Those who turn to socialism eventually turn away from God. Hitler said he just wanted to change economic priorities, but the first thing he did in office was to try to do away with Christianity. Stalin worked to rid the country of Christians. The Russians are socialistic, and they promote trusting the government and turning away from God.

Socialists turn the people away from God, the Bible, and Christian families. When you are building something on the Bible, you build it on faith in God, morality, and loyalty to your family. Christians live together and build something called a family.

The people in the family support each other. The family is the cornerstone of this country. Now we are moving in the wrong direction. Families are falling apart. About 70% of the children in America are not living with both of their birth parents. In so many instances in America, the family has been replaced by governmental support. The socialists want to completely take over our school systems. They want to do away with all private schools and teach all our children socialism. They want to do away with any prayers or Christian groups on the school property.

The father having leadership or authority in the home is a thing of the past. We are paying an awesome price for the government taking over. The children are getting into drugs and anarchy. They are looking for a leader in the local gang. If we don't turn these things around, our country will be destroyed. The Bible, the church, and the Lord Jesus is the only healing factor. Of course, the socialists are dead set against those three things.

We have numerous socialists in our government right now. Guess what will be hurt the most and the quickest if the socialists continue to take positions of leadership in our government? <u>Fifty-four percent of all discretionary spending by our government</u> is to build up our defense budget. The socialists would <u>love</u> it if our military was no longer the strongest military in the world.

After 70 years and the death of millions, the prison-house of communism and socialism burst open with the collapse of the Berlin Wall on November 9, 1989. The Union of Soviet Socialist Republic was dissolved and landed on the ash heap of history on Christmas Day 1991.

Socialism was in full rout. In the late 70's, socialist regimes had commanded the allegiance of some 60 percent of all people on earth. Socialism's spectacular crash in the years that followed signaled to many that this tragic and bloody experiment was at long last over.

The bitter experience with socialism showed millions ample evidence that collective ownership is just what one free market economist, Friedrich Hayek, called it in the 1940's, "The road to serfdom."

The record of socialism is lives lost, freedoms taken, and economies ruined. It shows how the envy-inflamed ideas of Marx, Engels, Lenin, Hitler, and many others are at war with the family, the church, and with God and His Word.

By cutting out God and emphasizing only human interaction, the early socialists began constructing systems aimed solely at raising the "poor classes" and thus bringing down the wealthy. Many of them stopped pretending that their vision was merely an advanced form of Christianity, and, like Karl Marx, embraced outright atheism.

Socialism takes away property and gives it to the government. Land is seized, major landowners are shot, and farming is collectivized under state supervision. The produce is taken by the state, which unilaterally sets farm workers' wages. Since there are no competing employers to bid for the workers' services, the workers have no choice but to accept what they are given. This is, of course, enslavement.

The claim that Scripture sides with socialism was dismissed more than 100 years ago by none other than Frederick Engels, co-author with Karl Marx of the Communist Manifesto. Engels believed that "if some few passages of the Bible may be similar to Communism, the general spirit of its doctrines is, nevertheless, totally opposed to socialism."

Even though Scripture is no friend to socialistic thought, some Christians still think it has a biblical basis. They point to the early church in Jerusalem which, at first glance, seems like a model socialist community. The author of Acts reports that these first believers "had all things in common" (Acts 4:32) and "all who were possessors of lands or houses sold them and brought the proceeds of the things that were sold and laid them at the apostles' feet; and they distributed to each as everyone had need" (Acts 4:34-35). <u>But unlike socialism, the sharing was voluntary, not coerced.</u>

Socialism has a heavy progressive or graduated income tax. They have an abolition of all rights of inheritance. They also confiscate all the property of all immigrants and rebels, and all private land is abolished.

Not only does socialism violate the eighth and tenth commandments against <u>theft</u> and <u>envy</u>, but it also violates the first commandment, "You shall have no other gods before me" (Exodus 20:3). Socialism seeks to play God, to take His place as the ultimate sovereign. After nearly 100 years, socialism has an unblemished record of failure. Wherever central planning and state control have taken the place of private ownership and market forces, the result has <u>always</u> been the same. A descent into poverty and atheism.

Why is socialism considered dangerous or bad for society as a whole? Socialism inhibits innovation and efficiency, the engines for economic growth, restricts the freedom of the individual, and provides a vehicle for corruption and tyrannical rule. Finally, socialism is costly and unsustainable.

The evil with socialism is that it will destroy your economic future—and your children's future; it creates an unjust society where a small political elite enriches itself by imposing a regime of equality of poverty and misery on most everyone else; and it has been associated with the worst crimes in human history.

As a minister, you have to know about and understand socialism. This is a horrible evil that is trying to get rid of Christianity. Be courageous and speak against it.

Senator Jim DeMint wrote a great book entitled, Saving Freedom. You ought to buy it and read it. The next few pages are the key ideas from that book.

Page 55. "People will not fight for freedom unless they understand it, value it, and believe it is at risk. Americans and freedom-loving people around the world must develop a deeper understanding and appreciation of freedom. To the oppressed, freedom may simply mean escape from their oppressors. To the poor, freedom may be the deliverance from want. To the anxious, freedom is synonymous with security.

These desires to be free from difficulty and danger are understandable, but they have led to a willingness to make government our master. Politicians with mostly good intentions have promised to help with more government solutions, but unless these leaders and policymakers develop a better understanding of freedom, their good intentions will continue to destroy not only our freedom but the very people they are trying to help.

Page 95. The implications of our national debt are complicated by the fact that a large and growing portion of our debt is held by foreign countries. Approximately $3 trillion of America's national debt is held by other countries, with China and Japan holding more than 40 percent of this debt. The biblical admonition from Proverbs certainly applies: 'The borrower is slave to the lender' (Proverbs 22:7). America's foreign policy and trade enforcement decisions are heavily influenced by our dependence on other countries to lend us more and more money. Because of our large and growing debt, America can no longer control its own destiny.

Page 130. Most textbook accounts of the birth of our nation now carefully ignore the religious aspect, as if a bunch of skeptics had written these famous lines from the Declaration of Independence: 'We hold these truths to be self-evident, that all men are created equal, that they are endowed by their

Creator with certain unalienable Rights, that among these are Life, Liberty, and the pursuit of Happiness.'

Page 131. An objective review of world and American history provides undeniable evidence that religion—far from being just a derivative of freedom—has been the primary catalyst and preserver of America's unique freedom and success."

Another book I would recommend for you to be able to knowledgeably speak against socialism is Truths About Socialism, written by the Coral Ridge Ministries.

This book tells the history of socialism and the horrible results it has left in every country where that philosophy ruled. I have listed some of the key points in the book for you to use in your ministry as you speak out against socialism.

Page 25. "Since the beginning of time, man has tried to replace God's authority with his own machinations, always with bad results. Socialism is man's prideful error on a gigantic scale.

Page 27. Socialism is an attempt to create heaven on earth according to an ever-changing morality fashioned by men themselves. Socialists are generally at war with the past; they believe that all that came before must be forgotten or destroyed in order to build a new Socialist Man from the ashes. This puts socialism at war, first and foremost, with

God and the Bible, and, indeed, with any religious faith that contains moral absolutes.

Page 125. Wherever Marxism and socialism have gained control, the Christian church has come under attack and suffered persecution.

The harsh reality is that socialism is at war with the true church of Jesus Christ. When socialists gain control, virtue, liberty, and religions are in great jeopardy.

Page 140-141. Jesus said, out of the heart a man speaks, (Luke 6:45) and socialism is an elaborate socio-economic structure that arises largely out of a heart of envy. It's not fair that you have more than I do. I want it (or at least some of it) and you must either give it or I'll take it from you—at the point of a gun. If it is the government pointing the gun, then I'm not morally culpable for taking it from you.

But socialism's lure goes even deeper than envy. By replacing God's rules with man's own, it frees man to pursue any vice he desires. So socialism is at bottom, a rebellion against God and God's clear words regarding morality and economics. That's why so many of the socialist philosophers were virulently atheist or tried to co-opt God in their versions of man-made paradise.

The problem is that when man becomes a law unto himself, he winds up under other men's tyranny. Unrestrained by the biblical, leveling notion of an Almighty God who will judge everyone's actions upon death, the makers of Heaven on

Earth will do anything to bring about their vision, up to and including theft, torture, and mass murder.

Christians and other people who value freedom face an enormous challenge if America is going to remain a self-governing, free nation. We must roll back the government before it becomes a god unto itself. And we must pray that God brings revival once again to us before it is too late."

The third book I would like to recommend to you is <u>The Case Against Socialism</u>, written by Senator Rand Paul. I wish every American would buy and read this book. The following quotes from this book will really help you.

Page 67. Rand Paul quotes a Cuban American who saw firsthand the horrors of socialism. He remained anonymous to protect his family still living in Cuba.

'When I hear of Bernie Sanders praising Castro, or see young people admiring Che Guevara, it makes me so angry.... how can you admire these criminals who killed thousands of people? People today are so uninformed about the horrors of socialism. I woke up one morning and the beautiful country I had known and loved was gone. The government had taken over all of the American and Cuban companies. Farmers were given twenty-four hours to leave their land....

You might get a 'free' education, but you have to study what the government tells you......Doctors make between $25 and $50 a month.... many professionals drive taxis in Cuba because they are tipped more in dollars from tourists than they can make at their professional jobs...."

And free health care? That is a joke! I know people in Cuba who have died from conditions that are completely treatable here in the United States. There is very little medicine available to the Cuban people so I send my family their prescription medications, even simple things like Band-Aids.

The idea that there is equality in Cuba is a lie—the people struggle for their basic needs while the government officials and those in the armed services live like kings!

The infrastructure is crumbling, and the streets are filled with potholes—except in the tourist areas. The government makes sure to present an attractive face to the rest of the world, but the regular neighborhoods are in terrible shape.'

Page 88. "In a 2015 speech at Harvard, Denmark's prime minister....said, 'I know that some people in the U.S. associate the Nordic model with some sort of socialism. Therefore, I would like to make one thing clear. Denmark is far from a socialist planned economy. Denmark is a market economy.'

Page 105. During the 1970s and '80s, Sweden drifted toward socialism and became one of the highest-taxed nations in the world. Tax revenues rose dramatically to consume 50 percent of Sweden's GDP. Denmark also saw taxes rise .... eventually also reaching 50 percent. Economic growth suffered and ever since that time, Scandinavian governments have been turning away from socialism.

Page 112. Millennials are shielded from the burden of taxes because most of them are part of the approximately half of the U.S. population that pays no income tax at all.

In the United States, the top 1 percent of income earners pays nearly 40 percent of the total income tax revenue, and the top 10 percent pay almost 70 percent. Meanwhile the bottom 50 percent of taxpayers paid only 3 percent of federal income tax in 2016. The upper middle class and the rich pay virtually all of the income tax in America and our tax code is already more progressive than that of Scandinavia.

Page 114. In recent elections, four out of five Nordic nations chose center-right governments. Wonder if someone should tell America's young socialists that not only is Scandinavia not socialist, but they seem to be heading back toward American capitalism."

Have you ever noticed that you have never seen people fleeing capitalism to seek a better future in a socialistic state? Everyone needs to understand that when you subsidize poverty and failure you get more of both.

If the socialists take over, they will immediately do all that they can to get rid of Christianity. The socialists want all of us to worship the government and not the Lord. There is a very clear historical record of this. If we do not take a stand soon, our churches will be destroyed, and our Christian leaders will be put in prison or killed.

In conversations with people, I have tried to convince them of the evil and horrific result on Christianity if socialism takes over our country. If they do not want to hear that, I try to help them understand the loss of freedom and financial destruction socialism generates.

As ministers, we have a responsibility to care for our people. Don't be cowardly. Pray that God will give you strength and wisdom as you speak against socialism. "[4] If you keep quiet at a time like this, deliverance and relief......will arise from some other place, but you and your relatives will die. Who knows if perhaps you were made.... for just such a time as this?" Esther 4:14 (New Living Translation)

I hope this book will help you. Please share it with other new ministers in your area. I hope this helps you to avoid making some of the mistakes that I made early in my ministry. Read Jeremiah 29:11 at least every other month. God bless you.

About the Author

Dr. Ron Churchill has been a minister for 56 years. He has a BA from Baylor University, Master's from Southwestern Baptist Theological Seminary, and a Doctorate from New Orleans Baptist Theological Seminary. Ron preached over 150 youth lead revivals in college and seminary while pastoring and working part time jobs. In addition, Ron completed Clinical Pastoral Education at Georgia Baptist Hospital.

Although most of his ministry was as the lead pastor, Dr. Churchill also held positions as BSU director as Southern Methodist University and was a single adult minister twice. As single adult pastor at Northway Baptist Church in Dallas, he grew a program from 150 single adults to over 900 within 4 years with over 25 giving their lives to full time Christian ministry. He has spoken for over 500 Single Adult Conferences and was the Keynote for Alabama State (1977) organizer and director of the first state wide Single Adult Conference in Georgia(1977), and conference leader (1978-1982) and Keynote (1982) for Texas State Singles. Dr. Churchill lead multiple meetings and conferences at Ridgecrest and Glorieta.

Dr. Churchill has written many articles for Southern Baptist Convention literature and magazines relating to single adult issues, leadership training, and church growth.

Dr. Churchill has been the lead pastor in seven churches. He pastored country churches, county seat churches, large-city

churches, small-city churches, and churches in and out of the Bible belt. He even pastored in a large retirement community. Regardless of the challenges each church had, they all doubled in size during his ministry. He pastored First Baptist Church of Plant City for over 21 years and that church not only doubled in membership but grew every year during his tenure to over 3,500 members. Dr. Churchill is uniquely gifted to teach other new ministers how to avoid mistakes and have a rewarding and growing ministry.

"Read this book and you will know the essentials of pastoral ministry, working with senior adults, single adults, and Sunday School classes. Dr. Churchill outlines in clever ways how to deal with difficult people, and how to help deacons and lay leadership become successful in the church's programs and ministries."

Dr. Page Fulgham Th.D.

www.ingramcontent.com/pod-product-compliance
Lightning Source LLC
Chambersburg PA
CBHW070721240426
43673CB00003B/93